Raising Kids in the 21st Century

Raising Kids in the 21st Century

The Science of Psychological Health for Children

Sharon K. Hall

WILEY-BLACKWELL

A John Wiley & Sons, Ltd., Publication

This edition first published 2008
© 2008 Sharon K. Hall

Blackwell Publishing was acquired by John Wiley & Sons in February 2007. Blackwell's publishing program has been merged with Wiley's global Scientific, Technical, and Medical business to form Wiley-Blackwell.

Registered Office
John Wiley & Sons Ltd, The Atrium, Southern Gate, Chichester, West Sussex, PO19 8SQ, United Kingdom

Editorial Offices
350 Main Street, Malden, MA 02148-5020, USA
9600 Garsington Road, Oxford, OX4 2DQ, UK
The Atrium, Southern Gate, Chichester, West Sussex, PO19 8SQ, UK

For details of our global editorial offices, for customer services, and for information about how to apply for permission to reuse the copyright material in this book please see our website at www.wiley.com/wiley-blackwell.

The right of Sharon K. Hall to be identified as the author of this work has been asserted in accordance with the Copyright, Designs and Patents Act 1988.

Library of Congress Cataloging-in-Publication Data

Hall, Sharon K.
    Raising kids in the 21st century : the science of psychological health for children / Sharon K. Hall.
        p.   cm.
    Includes bibliographical references and index.
    ISBN 978-1-4051-5806-0 (pbk. : alk. paper) – ISBN 978-1-4051-5805-3 (hardcover : alk. paper) 1. Child psychology. 2. Child development. 3. Child rearing. I. Title. II. Title: Raising kids in the twenty-first century.
    BF721.H225 2008
    649'.1019–dc22

                                                        2008009808

A catalogue record for this book is available from the British Library.

Set in 10.5/13pt Sabon by SPi Publisher Services, Pondicherry, India

1   2008

This book is dedicated to Alex, who explores the world with an open heart and gives me hope for the children of the 21st century.

Contents

Preface

◆　◆　◆

When I discuss children and development with my students they often ask me how long have psychologists known about certain aspects and why don't *they* know such valuable information. I tell them that I believe psychologists and educators need to get their research into the general public's hands more often. Our science has so much to offer parents and teachers in practical terms. Another point that my students often make in class is that the reading of research in texts does not easily translate to the applications of the material. Well said! There are many strong textbooks about child and adolescent development. Yet information that could be used on a daily basis needs a bridge, a link between the scientific and popular psychology that would be useful to parents, teachers, and students.

There is a rich database of research on how to raise psychologically healthy children. The goal of this book is to distill those findings for those new to psychology or for lay people to help them apply this knowledge to the benefit of their families. Other books directed toward applications of parenting and family study are often not based in science. While some of these books are popular and/or interesting, they are often based on a few clinical case studies or the authors' own childhoods. Much is known among academics about the socialization of healthy children, but these ideas are rarely translated so that a larger reading audience may benefit from them.

My vision for writing this book was to translate to others what is known about the socialization of healthy children. In this book I have tied the science, the practice, and the fun of raising psychologically healthy children. My hope is that people who are or who will become parents and teachers will enjoy the vignettes, be stimulated by the science, and feel empowered to use the science in their daily lives with the help of the guidelines I provide.

Within this book you will read about research from some of the giants in the developmental child literature. Researchers such as James Comer, Diane Halpern, Reed Larson, and Ann Masten have much to tell us about children's psychological health and how whole communities can be responsible for their welfare. Constance Flanagan tells us that as we mentor engaged, happy children, we are creating a virtuous circle. These children will become our social activists and work within their communities and the globe to enrich our world.

I wish to acknowledge all of the researchers whose work has inspired me to share a great deal of what is known in the developmental psychology literature with students, parents, teachers, and all adults whose lives are enriched by children. Particular thanks are given to my students who show their curiosity about and concern for children and whose questions compelled me to translate this research for the consumption of many.

I offer thanks to Chris Cardone, Sarah Coleman, and Kelly Basner at Blackwell for their unflagging support and editorial assistance. I am also grateful to the reviewers who provided their feedback with aplomb, to Laura Hartrick and Virginia Randall for their assistance with the manuscript, and to Jim, whose support is daily.

Chapter 1

Raising Kids in the 21st Century

◆ ◆ ◆

The scene on the home video opens with a two year old dancing and singing along with a musical number from the movie *Mary Poppins* called "Step in Time." The characters the child is watching are vibrant, exciting, and fun. The dancing toddler stops to smile at the camera, says "Daddy steptime!" and waves to her father to join her. The camera held by the mother continues to record as the father enters the scene, hugs and kisses his child, then begins to dance and sing. All three are laughing and are in this moment of gaiety together. How did this child develop into such an active, happy person, obviously connected to two adults who adore her? I will take you on a journey of discovery that will help to answer this question and show you how this family scene is possible for everyone.

Healthy children are our goal. There are two kinds of health we should tend to, however: physical *and* psychological. Many parents understand the importance of a physically healthy child. For example, we know that pregnancy requires women to take care of their bodies in order for the child to be healthy. After birth, we watch children's development very closely for behaviors like their first steps and their first words. Physicians and other health care providers remind us of the importance of immunizations and yearly check-ups. Many people are interested in children's health. We see them as our future.

However, promoting the *psychological* health of children is less understood. Goals or targets of psychological health are not discussed to the extent that physical health needs are in families. While most parents might know that young children need their physical care, the emotional bonds and relationships of parents and children are the foundation upon which the children's psychological health is built. These building blocks mean that adults are helping children to develop into the parents, teachers, and community leaders of tomorrow. Psychological health contributes to their futures as well as that of our world. Strong communities are built upon active, involved, committed people who understand that relationships are keys to progress and that responsibility for the future begins with the individual.

What do you think psychological health in children looks like? You can likely think of two or three good goals. You probably know that we can expect children to get along well with others, to be able to go to school without a lot of distress, and that they will eventually take some responsibility for their own actions. These are all wonderful goals that many children realize, but do you know how to promote these goals? Promoting this kind of psychological health is possible and needs discussion so that adults are well informed and ready for the challenges ahead. Are there other goals of emotional and social skill-building that are linked with psychological health? Yes, adults such as parents and teachers show children how to go forth into their environments with skill and a desire for connecting with others every day. This skill is also called *social competence* by psychologists and simply means a set of positive social behaviors that have been mastered with the likelihood that the child can use this skill in the future as well. Small steps toward social competence made with loving encouragement are as important for building psychological health as those first steps around the room are markers of physical health.

My purpose for writing this book is to show the reader how building healthy relationships with the children in our lives helps them become healthy people psychologically. This facilitation of healthy development is also called "scaffolding," a word used by the Russian psychologist Lev Vygotsky (1962) to describe supporting children's learning. Consider a structure going up and note the scaffolding used to facilitate the building on that site. So too do adults scaffold the development of children by providing a framework the children can use to grow in their environments. Healthy, happy people who can connect well with others, see others' perspectives with tolerance, and care about their world are possible with the right foundation. Psychology can help us do this important work.

Because I refer to psychological health often, I have decided to use the term "Ph" to stand for that phrase. It reminds us that our psychological health is related to our physical health also. Recall that the use of the term "good Ph" means that balance of acid and alkaline in our physical world. For this book, a good Ph will mean that balance of building relationships with personal responsibility. This concept simply means that adults nurture children every day and this includes teaching them responsibility for their actions, that their actions have consequences, and that we expect them to develop within the limits of this framework to help them become healthy children psychologically.

Another parameter that will be used in this book concerns the use of the pronouns "he" and "she." These pronouns will be alternated by chapter, so that, for example, when referring to a child in chapter 1, the pronoun "she" will be used, while in chapter 2, the pronoun "he" will be used, and so on. This is very important so that the reader can think of these concepts about good Ph for both girls and boys. If psychologists have found that girls and boys differ in an important way, this will be delineated appropriately, as well.

One caveat for the reader to consider is the concept of "normal development." Psychologists have studied children to the extent that we know at about what age certain skills should be developing or mastered. This means that the majority of children we have studied are able to use the skill at the age we describe. This does not mean that all children fit this mold. The age groups are simply there to help us understand development across many children. Psychologists establish this average through several studies and then report their findings. However, one caveat is especially important to consider as we begin. Much of what is known about normal development and families is based on white, middle-class people.

The interplay of factors such as cultural and ethnic backgrounds, economics, physical ability, and sexual orientation are not well studied. "Normal development" is used as a phrase to describe all children, but the reality is, we are only just now examining the full lives of children from various backgrounds. This means that much of this book is about expectations for and the development of children from white, middle-class families. There will be some discussion about studies richer in dimensions like that of ethnicity, but overall, every reader should keep this caveat in mind as the book progresses. Remember that human variation is what makes us complex and fascinating, and that a large part of psychological science concerns the discovery of this variation.

Building Blocks of Psychological Health

In the early years of a child's development psychologists have historically looked at two concepts that merit some discussion here. Both "temperament" and "self-regulation" have been found to be good predictors of later outcomes for children. In psychology, we refer to temperament as a construct consisting of the children's characteristics as they respond to the environment. The characteristics that are often studied in infants are excitability, activity level, social responsiveness, and motivation. Many psychologists believe that children are born with a tendency toward ease or excitability and interest in their environments. We make estimates about their temperament by noting their physical activity levels and desire to be with others. Healthy adult caregivers must respond to the "easy children" and the "excitable children" with the goals of healthy child outcomes in mind. Another construct related to temperament is the extent to which very young children learn to self-regulate their physical, emotional, and social responses to their environments. "Self-regulation" means that children have a set of skills such as control over their focus or attention, an ability to calm themselves when tended to by adults, and then later, control of their own behavior.

While this discussion about temperament and self-regulation may seem to place the child as the focus, healthy relationships with adult caregivers is the children's key to mastering their environments. These interactions begin with a concept that psychologists call "goodness of fit." Goodness of fit means that the interactions of parents and children seem to flow rather smoothly. When adults are competent, functioning caregivers, they can respond appropriately to "easy" or "excitable" children and assist the children with their development. For example, a usually high-energy mother may note that she must lower her voice when attending to her excitable, physically active infant in order to help calm the baby. Conversely, a very calm mother may note that she must bring her physical activity level up with her very easy and calm infant in order to stimulate the baby's interest in the environment. In both instances the goodness of fit concept demonstrates that, although the mothers' characteristics are not in sync with the babies' needs automatically, both are willing to shift to help their children develop. Children's good Ph is reliant on sensitive stimulation by caring adults at birth and beyond.

Below you will find lists that concern the building blocks of good Ph. Psychologists know that a progression of skill-building usually occurs over the lifespan and this is considered normal development. These expectations for each age group are listed in the order psychologists have found they develop in children, starting from birth. This first group of relationship-building and personal responsibility skills occurs from birth to two years of age. These are simply behaviors that children should be practicing and mastering over the first two years.

Ph list for first two years of life
1   Brings the caregiver to her, often with crying, when she's in need of food, comfort, and safety.
2   Responds with eye contact and audible sounds of pleasure or relaxation when tended or satiated.
3   Physically calms own body movements after attention.
4   Effort to bring desired objects close to the body for play.
5   Effort to repeat sounds, turn-taking begins with verbal sounds.
6   Babbling and cooing that begins to sound like language.
7   Communication is desired and attempted. One-word "sentences" to communicate by age one develops into two- and three-word sentences by 18 months.
8   Has confidence in one or two caregivers and is shy or frightened of others. Uses caregiver as "secure base" for exploration. More comfortable with others by age two.
9   Learning rules of the home, what is allowed, the limits and consequences of her actions as an independent person from others.
10   Observing others as models of behavior: parents, siblings, teachers, peers, etc.

This progression has occurred by the time the child is two years of age!

Let us look at what develops in the years called "early childhood." This period is also referred to as the "preschool years," from ages two to five or two to six.

Ph list for early childhood

1 Eye and hand coordination develops so that small tasks are possible. Dressing oneself and taking one's dishes to the sink are examples of simple tasks that show some independence and competence.

2 Seeks mastery. Has some awareness that independence and competence feel good.

3 Vocabulary increases a lot during this period. Communication is skilled by school age.

4 Ability to focus on longer tasks develops, that is, attention span increases.

5 Playmates are noted and desired. Around two, play means sitting beside a friend for company. By age five or six, play that is coordinated with another is desired. Complex games emerge.

6 Social relationships are building. Parental modeling of caring connections is noted and repeated.

7 Some conflict-resolution skill, but the child's emotional control likely still needs adult intervention at times. Rate of conflict should diminish by age six.

8 Moderate amount of comfort with the social world that now includes other adults as well as other children. This larger network of people means that the child must begin to generalize what she knows about getting along at home to the larger context of school, playgrounds, and such.

9 Affect control is more mature by age six. Trials of skinned knees or hurt feelings may still draw out a tearful response, but overall, the school-aged child can monitor and control feelings to some extent.

10 Desire for pleasing adults and being recognized as a competent person is strong.

Wow! The school-aged child is ready for the world.

Let's turn now to the middle years of childhood, which include those first years in the elementary grades of school. The ages associated with this period are six to twelve.

Ph list for middle childhood

1 Understanding of the physical world develops rapidly, and along with it, social skills. New concepts and associations help the child see herself in many settings and in relationships.

2 Developing concepts like "perspective-taking" help the child learn that others have different opinions and feelings that need attention for building relationships.
3 Developing the ability to focus on more than one aspect of a situation at one time is related to perspective-taking.
4 Reflecting on the self as a competent person with choices to make.
5 Developing language skill and considering how to use it effectively. Word games and puns are fun!
6 Increases in memory mean that organizing information and being able to use it when needed are effective tools in building and maintaining relationships at home and at school.
7 Peers include boys and girls, but each sex often prefers same-sex friendships.
8 Thinking about the future emerges such that careers and marriage are considered.
9 Grapples with what it means to be a good friend. Loyalty, commitment, and kindness developing with close friends.
10 Physical aggression with peers overall has diminished, but hostile verbal aggression can increase.

The next period of development is called "adolescence," which includes the years from ages twelve to twenty. As psychologists have learned more about the adolescent period, we have found two groups that seem to share characteristics more easily delineated than just "adolescents." We call the two groups "Early Adolescence" and "Late Adolescence."

Think of the list below as in a chronological order, as usual. However, the first five tasks more likely emerge in early adolescence, the second five in late adolescence. As with all of the discussion thus far, children can develop some skills earlier or later than the guidelines that are provided. However, the majority of children develop skills at the rates listed below.

Ph list for adolescence
1 Physical changes of puberty that include hormone shifts. These physical changes mean emotional uncertainty also.
2 Thinking skill has become more complex so that self-reflection is a daily occurrence.

3   Responsibility and relationships are considered frequently.
4   Increasing competence in all areas helps provide a good feeling about the self.
5   Considering many alternatives for solutions in a systematic way is emerging.
6   Insight about the self includes abilities and desires for further development.
7   Friendship groups of boys and girls devolve into boy/girl pairs and dating.
8   Dating relationships are reflections of early behavior with friends. Characteristics like honesty and loyalty are evident.
9   Planning for the future includes family and career goals that will continue to develop over the next decade.
10 Relationship responsibility is evident and is seen across all interactions, school groups, work, community, etc.

These skill expectations are not exhaustive but give an overall picture of the skills children need to become functioning adults. The good Ph path begins early. The balance of relationships and personal responsibility is needed for healthy outcomes, but not all children will achieve these competencies for various reasons. Families can be sorely taxed with chronic problems such as poverty, unemployment, drug addiction, etc. or by severe traumas that may occur only once, yet have a lasting impact on the development of children. For those children who begin in vulnerable families, there is still much hope because of the possibility of early positive relationships with caregivers, despite the hurdles. A review of the concept of resilience is a good place to begin this discussion.

Resilience and Psychological Health

Resilience is that quality people are said to possess who develop well, despite adversity or even great odds. What is known about resilience began with the study of positive psychology as a concept in the last few decades of the 20th century. Psychologists Martin Seligman (1991) and Mihaly Csikszentmihalyi (Csikszentmihalyi and Beattie 1979) began to understand that previous research more often focused on pathology or human behavior that needed intervention. This is not too surprising, given the nature of the field in general. Psychologists hoped to understand human behavior so that social or personal ills could be ameliorated. Beginning in the 1970s and 1980s, researchers such as Michael Rutter (1979) and Norman Garmezy (1985) were writing about the need for examining those children who are psychologically healthy, despite risks such as poverty. In their early work, they found that a few factors stood out as those associated with the children who faced risk but had good outcomes. These factors were a positive temperament, a normal level of intelligence, one good parent, one good external resource such as a teacher, and one positive context external to the home such as a well-functioning school. Many researchers call these "protective factors" that lead to resilience.

More recently, developmental psychologist Ann Masten (Masten and Coatsworth 1998), her colleagues, and others have extended these early findings such that we now have a framework of factors that are associated with resilient children. With this more recent research, we know that along with a normal intelligence level and biological integrity, the facets of temperament that are associated with resilience include an easygoing, sociable disposition and a belief in one's ability to master the environment, getting along with others, and having good self-esteem. Resilient children often have families who include one good parent with warmth and high expectations, as well as positive relationships with extended family members. Further, socioeconomic stability and advantage are associated with families who have resilient children despite difficulties. Outside of the family, one positive, involved adult has been associated with a favorable outcome for the child through schools, and religious or secular organizations. Masten and Coatsworth summarized these details about the construct of resilience in 1998 and these factors are still being studied today. Note that because of the nature of the research, a line of causality from protective factors leading to resilience has not been established. However, we know the factors *associated* with good outcomes. It is possible for children to adapt to challenges in their environments. This adaptation we call resilience is extremely reliant on social relationships. The role of parents in the building of resilience looks huge, but others external to the family can have positive associations with children as well. Competent teachers from positive school environments are also key to children's good Ph.

Parents are the foundation of all social relationships. Indeed, Masten and Coatsworth state that strengthening the parent-child bond "is a key strategy for intervention" when we wish to promote adaptation in children. Resilience in the face of adversity is possible for children, and healthy outcomes are associated with the scaffolding of positive relationships in place. It is also the case that families experience chronic and acute hurdles that are associated with child outcomes. Psychologists call these hurdles "risk." For example, poverty is one chronic risk factor for children, while one natural disaster experience such as a hurricane would be an acute risk factor for poor outcomes. These risk factors to normal development mean that children can be vulnerable to poor outcomes.

When risk occurs in families, whether chronic or acute, the parents' response is observed by children as cues about how to manage their own response. Psychologists have studied parents who raise children with vulnerabilities inherent to the family such as chronic poverty or divorce, yet their children become thriving, successful adults. Hallmarks of these families include inculcation of certain values like the importance of family relationships, individual responsibility, and high academic expectations. For example, child psychiatrist James Comer of Yale University found in his studies with ethnic minority children that strong families and schools can help children overcome very high risk factors such as prejudice and discrimination (see Comer 2004). Further, we also know that when families encounter risk factors to children's good Ph that include life-threatening events or trauma, many children can cope with the help of their families as well.

The research on children who have experienced a one-time only or acute trauma is nascent. However, one finding that has been repeated is that parents' ability to provide warmth and feelings of safety to their children after trauma predicts the children's coping Thus, parental coping is believed to be the best predictor of children's coping after a traumatic event. For example, psychologist A. C. McFarlane (1988) followed a group of children who had experienced a natural disaster in Australia. He found that the mother's reactions to the event were better predictors of the children's responses than even the children's proximity to the destructive event. Results like these have been found with children from the Middle East and the United States who have also experienced trauma. Fortunately, trauma researchers have found that other caring adults may provide this kind of protective factor as well. Psychologist George A. Bonanno, who has conducted numerous studies on post-trauma resilience, states that there are many paths to recovery after trauma (see Bonanno 2004). Individual resilience is one of those pathways that really look like collaborations between people after all.

Supporting children's healthy psychological development is possible as families and whole communities focus on the protective factors that make a difference in children's lives. We know that building children's resilience to risk is possible and that healthy Ph can be an outcome for many children. A focus on children's development of cognitive, social, and emotional health translates into psychological health that should be a goal with as much emphasis as that presently seen in the United States for physical health. While the tasks vary as children develop, the adults' role to serve as caregivers and teachers remains prominent for the rearing of psychologically healthy children.

The Book to Come

The emphasis of this book is on building relationships and the development of personal responsibility for good Ph and how these are associated with positive outcomes for children as adults. We will begin by looking at cognitive growth in the home and in environments external to the home, such as formal childcare and schooling. Social growth at home and with peers will follow a similar path. The process of how children develop their values and their relationship to others will be examined along with their development of humor. In the last chapter, the role of cognitive growth and social growth, including values and humor in relationships, will be presented as good predictors of a psychologically healthy life, full of social activism. These concepts will be linked to a developing dialogue about promoting tolerance as a part of good Ph.

The dancing toddler in the opening vignette looks as though her developmental course has been laid with a solid foundation, one with protective factors in place that will assist her as she grows. Her parents are showing her how healthy relationships lead to good Ph that will benefit others in the years to come. Good Ph begins with cognitive and social growth in the home.

Chapter 2

Early Cognitive Growth

◆ ◆ ◆

The infant whose eyes are beautiful, but yet to focus, is ready to nurse. The mother prepares to nurse her baby, coos and talks while she is settling both into the chair, relaxes and begins. The baby looks at her – *really* looks at her and studies her face, closes his eyes and calms himself to nurse. The mother is ecstatic; the moment is new and wonderful. Her baby's focus is evident; he is calmed and nourished by her presence. The mother knows her baby has begun a series of cognitive changes that will connect him with her and to the world.

In this chapter we will consider the first measure for good Ph: the development of cognitive skills in early childhood. Cognitive development or growth simply means the development of children's thinking over time. How well people interact with their environments depends a lot upon how well they remember things learned in the past, how they use their knowledge to go about a normal day successfully, and how well they examine new information and incorporate the novel into their repertoire of knowledge. I will explore the markers of normal cognitive growth as they relate to good Ph and to good parenting. As discussed in chapter 1, normal growth is that mastery of skills which research has shown most children can accomplish by a particular age.

Good Ph is promoted when children have a solid beginning in their first learning environments. The first interactions infants have with the adults in their lives give them information about how their environments are characterized in general. How adults respond to infants is a very important precursor of how the children will grow in the years to come. The range of responses of adult caregivers to children can be very wide indeed. Some infants have caregivers who meet all of their needs with attention and love; other infants have no attention given to them by adults. Many other infants receive adult care at some point in between the two anchors of this continuum of care and connection.

Children's thinking begins developing in their physical environments the day of their births. Even prior to birth, researchers believe that children's cognitions are mostly reflexive, but they do respond to the outside environment. The newborn's physical needs require dyadic interactions immediately and these are infinitely intertwined with cognitive and social development. The normal infant calls to adults for care by crying, relaxes when satiated, and desires human contact. Eye contact is evident by three months of age and in conjunction with crying, smiling, and cooing, is an indicator of expected, needed physical care and concern by caregivers. The journey of human relationships begins early and continues throughout children's development. This early cognitive growth is crucial for good Ph.

My goal in this chapter is to demonstrate how young children's cognitive development progresses and how adults can stimulate this growth. We will begin by exploring the nature of adult-infant interactions and then examine what can happen when this bond is tenuous or mostly nonexistent. Cognitive growth develops in tandem with social skill. This interaction of domains of development is not surprising. Social functioning is related to cognitive functioning and both are needed for good Ph. Psychological health requires that a solid foundation of adult attention be established in order for children to develop and maintain an interest in their environments. This interest eventually translates into the infants' own active manipulations of the physical world that assist in their cognitive development. Infants actively construct their own development, albeit along with much assistance from the adults in their lives.

Background and Research

The infant has great interest in the world around him. For caregivers who are able to provide stimulation to their children, the rewards are great. This stimulation can be in the form of toys, books, music, touch, and other human faces and voices. The infant who manipulates a toy is learning many new things. Stimulating infants' cognitive growth is probably one of the most published topics that parents may tap in the popular media.

In the 1970s and 1980s there was much media attention concerning the extent to which middle- and upper-class parents could stimulate the cognitive growth of their children. The information in the popular media about how to provide children cognitive stimulation was often correct, but took on a tone of overdoing a good thing. Much emphasis was placed upon skill development, such as visual recognition of shapes and placing objects into categories as a form of cognitive stimulation in order to raise "bright" children. Timelines and schedules were provided to parents as the optimum stimulation courses needed for raising intellectually gifted infants. While some infants may have benefited from this zealotry, a cautionary note concerns the nature of the overall development of children and the extent to which infants tolerate stimulation.

A loving parent who stimulates an infant with regard for the infant's comfort is also giving the child information about his environment and important others in it. The child's comfort and interest in the stimulating moments should be the focus of adult intervention, not raising genius children. Social and cognitive skill development occur together. Infants rely on their caregivers to provide a sensitive environment that includes appropriate levels of stimulation for cognitive growth. The caregiver whose focus on the infant's optimum development includes sensitivity and nurturing along with cognitive stimulation is helping to promote overall psychological health.

What do we know about infant cognition? Renowned infant cognition psychologist Elizabeth S. Spelke (2002) has found that infant cognition is complex, despite the difficulties in researching infant thought without the benefit of their use of verbal language. Such "nonlinguistic representation" in the infant means that carrying out research on this developmental stage of life can be a challenge. Yet, Spelke and researchers like her have found that infants have concepts of objects, a rudimentary concept of cause and effect, can recognize people who care for them, and can distinguish one from many objects, to name a few before the age of one year. While not all psychologists agree about the depth of infant cognition, these findings along with many others show that much is going on in the infant's cognitive world. In this regard infant cognition is rich and multidimensional.

Physical Health

It is important to remember the dependence infants have on the adult world for their biological needs, as well. First, the infant's physical world must include food, warmth, and comfort. Adults provide these basic needs so that the baby's physical development proceeds along a healthy course. Further, the baby's lack of physical distress means that he can attend to environmental stimulation. Several decades of research in psychology and infant development have shown that physically healthy babies function well cognitively, compared to those infants whose physical health is compromised by low birth weight, lack of nutrition, or neglect related to psychological factors such as, for example, an unwanted pregnancy.

Indeed, infant cognition researchers such as Susan A. Rose (1994) have shown that among infants who are underweight, behaviors like visual recognition and the coordination of visual stimuli to touch are less well developed than the same behaviors in heavier babies, and this difference is evident as early as five months of age. A physically healthy infant has a good chance of adapting well to the environment with the assistance of social relationships. The infant who is born with an average weight and who has his nutritional needs met by adult caregivers is usually skilled at this adaptation. All infants need a solid basis of physical health in order to develop socially and cognitively. Remember the notes in chapter 1 about the interaction of the physical with the psychological world? Both are needed for normal development to progress. Good Ph is promoted by the intersection of physical, cognitive, and socio-emotional health.

Cognitive Baby Steps

One example of an infant's attempts to manipulate the environment is a good starting point for discussion of specific behaviors necessary for the infant's cognitive development to progress. An infant sees an object in his visual field. With sweeping, uncoordinated arm movements, he attempts to pull this object to his body. One day, after several tries, the baby succeeds in sweeping this object to his body. The object pulled into proximity by the baby can then be seen more clearly and batted about. With further attempts, the baby can pick up an object that he has pulled into his proximity. The held object can then be manipulated even more. The object can be dropped, observed some more, perhaps picked up again by the baby. While this progression occurs over the first nine months of the infant's life, it is remarkable to watch and actually occurs quite rapidly.

As the baby learns to manipulate one object, rudimentary rules about the object are noted. Sounds come out of the rattle when it is shaken, so the infant shakes it some more. The baby in the example delights in manipulating the toy and may give it a good toss away from his body, whether from excitement or some more purposive action. Although psychologists cannot say to what extent the baby's cognitive representation of an event includes "Sometimes when I throw it I can't get it back," the baby may become distressed at this point and call the caregiver to him for assistance. This event often means that an adult must engage in the game of picking up the object and getting it back to the baby's proximity, perhaps over and over again.

Many wonderful underpinnings of these seemingly everyday attempts at mastery in the lives of babies occur prior to these first manipulations of the environment. These underpinnings or approximations of skill development occur in fairly predictable order and are the essence of the developing child.

Mastery Achieved

For an infant to "conquer" pulling a desired object into the body like the child in our example, several behaviors on the part of the infant are required. Further, all require coordinating efforts into a pattern of behavior that might be called a "mastery skill set." The various behaviors evident in the conquering infant are myriad and perhaps surprising to those who do not study infant development. The progression from the infant's extreme dependence as a neonate without locomotion or coordinated movement to the physical manipulation of the environment occurs over the first year of life. The following is a summary list of the functioning evident in the successful infant who learns to manipulate objects and draw the caregiver in for a game of "Pick up my toy!"

Mastery skill set for early exploration
1   Visual focus.
2   Attention.
3   Physically adept at gross motor movement.
4   Interest/desires stimulation.
5   Recognition of a desired object.
6   Novelty excitement.
7   Perseverance of focus and action.
8   Coordination of visual, touch, and motor behaviors.
9   Some coordination of opposing thumb and fingers.
10 Pre-language vocalizations of emotions that draw caregivers to
    the infant, for example, excitement, frustration.

Voila! The infant has the toy, drops it, and vocalizes so that adults
know it is time for some assistance, some play. "Pick up my toy!" has
begun. The infant's mastery skill set is evident and includes the caregiver or social other in the game.

The Language of Emotion

A big part of adults' willingness to engage in this reciprocal behavior
concerns the extent to which the infant's behaviors include a desire
for human contact. When healthy infants enter the world, they are
capable of making facial expressions and sounds, they can see objects
and people, they can hear, smell, and touch. The acuity of these senses
varies, but they are present in the newborn nonetheless. All of these
functions help infants to adapt to their new environments. Psychologists
such as infant researcher Robert Emde (1980) state that the interaction of biology and social development is crucial for cognitive adaptation. The infant's ability to express emotions is a universally adaptive
behavior that facilitates adults' interest in the newborn. Across cultures and socio-demographic circumstances, infant emotion requires
a response by caring adults in their lives. By the age of two months,
infants are also interested in adults and engage in significant amounts
of face scanning of their caregivers. At this two-month juncture,
infants have shifted from solely emotional responses to their own
internal states, to include responding to the environment, and the
people in it. The nursing baby in this chapter's opening paragraph had

likely achieved this emotional focus shift. His focus on his mother, even for a few seconds, meant that he was responding to something in his environment.

Emotional expressions evident in the infant by six months include the cry, smile, interest, surprise, fear, anger, and sadness. What a very large repertoire of expression for such a small person! While language will quickly become another mode of communication, these early signals from the infant to the caregiver are considered to be crucial for good Ph to develop. The parent and infant bond is developing through the language of emotional expression. These early exchanges of information are the precursors to language and other cognitive and social development.

Hanus and Mechthild Papousek (1992) – experts in the field of infants' emotional expression and cognition – believe that adults' ability to stimulate their infants is genetically programmed, or adaptive and unconscious. Adults have adaptive messages from their genes about nurturing their infants and most caregivers perform this function. For healthy parent and infant pairs, the psychological bond is building. The Papouseks state that the stimulation of infants must occur within some fairly narrow boundaries in order for infant cognition to develop, however. In order for infants to respond to stimuli, the following limits provide a positive framework for growth:

Stimulating infant cognition
1   Infants must be presented with fairly simple stimuli: one object at a time by one person at a time.
2   Infants need repetition of simple stimuli.
3   Infants' tolerance for stimuli must be deciphered and respected for their optimal attention and comfort.
4   Infants respond to a hierarchy of skill development. For example, when a baby emits a sound such as "D," the parent can respond. The parent may stimulate the infant to pair this with a vowel sound by saying a phrase such as "Say Da, Daddy."
5   Infant feedback about the progression in skills must be followed. For example, when the infant exhibits some mastery with one sound, caregivers can stimulate the production of other sounds systematically.

These behaviors on the part of parents are believed to be universal across cultures, sex, and age. People other than biological parents who engage in the above behaviors are also successful at facilitating infant cognition. These behaviors can be considered scaffolds or support to the infant's cognitive development. This support may be provided by older siblings, other relatives, or childcare workers as well.

Parent-Child Reciprocity

Adults, often parents and childcare workers in the infants' world, provide the environment the young child will develop in. The interactions adults have with children, whether through face-to-face contact or by simply placing interesting objects into the children's environment, are predictors of the children's later competence. The role of the adult caregiver cannot be minimized. A group of researchers who were charged with examining parental care and other childcare on the behalf of the National Institute of Child Health and Human Development (NICHD) had this to say:

> Parenting is a major predictor of children's cognitive and social development because of the centrality of the family in children's early lives and because it includes positive genetic as well as environmental influences on the children. (Network 2006: 100)

These psychologists went on to say that quality childcare outside of the home is also related to positive gains in language and other cognitive and social development. (I will discuss childcare and cognitive development more comprehensively in chapter 3.) Note that the NICHD research group stresses both genetics from the parents and the environmental influences that parents provide in their assertion about the importance of parents in children's development. "Positive genetics" refers to the expression of genes in healthy infants that help set the course for their development. For example, those infants who are interested in their environments and who can calm themselves with some assistance by caregivers are thought to have a positive temperament, a characteristic associated with a genetic predisposition to respond to the environment. Remember that this self-regulating behavior was discussed in chapter 1 and is related to cognitive and social interactions as well.

A healthy infant who can call the caregiver to him and be satiated, calmed, and satisfied within a reasonable amount of time will likely adapt well to the environment both as an infant and in future development. This reciprocity or exchange of information between infants and caregivers helps to insure that the infant develops normally. Remember that the genetic predisposition for parents to nurture their offspring is considered an adaptive function that other primates in the animal kingdom engage in also. Those adults who involve their infants in the world with sensitivity to the children's needs are stimulating their cognitive growth. Not all parent-infant dyads begin so positively, however, so research on compromised development is important to examine as well.

Risk and Resilience

Researchers in psychology have studied groups of children whose beginnings were compromised, their early development thwarted such that normal developmental progressions did not occur. Two such studies concern children from the island of Kauai, Hawaii and from Romania. However, from both studies we will also see that some children have difficulty with risk factors at birth and in their families, while other children can be resilient and thrive.

Infant vulnerability is great in that their dependence on adult caregivers is also great. Adults can lack functioning because of factors such as poverty, mental illness, alcoholism, or loss through traumatic events. Children from Kauai who had family risk factors like these were at increased risk of less than normal functioning as adults. Some children such as those from the Romanian orphanages had very little care from any adults until they were adopted. However, in some ways, very young infants are also protected from early negative life factors because of their lack of memory for and understanding of the negative events. Further, many children at risk for poor cognitive outcomes can "catch up." Nonetheless, a look at the hurdles some infants face and their outcomes helps us to better understand normal development.

A study of infants from Kauai was conducted by psychologists Emmy E. Werner and Ruth S. Smith (1982) over a thirty-year period. Such a "longitudinal" study – research conducted over a period of time with one group of people – often yields some phenomenal data. The children were seen as infants and studied at different intervals until they were about 31 years of age. Approximately 16 percent of all of these infants had a handicap at birth or difficulty during the birthing process that meant their development could be thwarted or require some form of intervention, for example, cognitive remediation in school. These developmental deficits included physical abnormalities or a compromised intelligence level. Among these high risk infants at birth, about two-thirds developed serious learning or behavioral problems by the time they were ten years of age. However, these children's lives were also characterized by other risk factors along with their own cognitive or physical impairments. This other risk factor was most often the family environment.

Families living in chronic poverty with a lack of permanence in the household, including mental illness of a parent, were more likely those with the impaired children who were not coping well with adulthood at age 31. The rearing conditions present in these children's lives meant that their success in school was thwarted, their own mental health compromised, and their ability to become functioning adults lessened. By the young age of two, these children's cognitive and social growth was vulnerable, due to environmental risk factors in their lives. Parental discord, divorce, alcoholism, or mental illness contributed to these children's development of serious learning or behavioral deficits by age ten. These same precursors meant that these children had higher rates of delinquency, school failure, mental health problems, or adolescent pregnancies by age eighteen. Early, positive parent-child interactions that are so important to overall development did not occur. The amount of stimulation and nurturing some of the children received from their parents was not enough to help them overcome the challenges presented to them at birth and by their family environments.

Interestingly, one-third of these Kauai children at risk for poor outcomes were resilient in terms of the hurdles they faced. How did the resilient children become so? Werner and Smith found that those same qualities or protective factors that were discussed in chapter 1 concerning resilience were true. The children who were active and alert physically and who could be calmed by a caregiver were thought to have a positive social orientation. This social orientation meant that a close bond with one caregiver was possible. The parents were sensitive to the needs of their children. This same parent-infant bond was seen as a good starting point for structure, rules, and assigned chores as the children developed. These children also had one strong external support during their adolescent years, whether through schools, neighborhoods, or religious contexts. The competent parents who provided their impaired child with a stable family life, even in the face of adversity, were able to assist their children in their successful journey to adulthood. According to these findings about the children of Kauai and their competent parents, resilience in the face of adversity is possible.

And what of the children reared in Romanian orphanages? Many of these children were abandoned by their parents during a horrific period of history in Romania. The government demanded that adults have large families, but provided no economic stability for families to flourish. Rather, families were starving to death. The children were left in orphanages that were neither equipped nor funded to provide for their developmental needs. The children more often had only a roof over their heads, without heat, appropriate nutrition, or adult interest and care. These risk factors together can be described by the phrase "early, severe deprivation." Their basic needs were not met. The adult-infant bond necessary for the development of good Ph was nonexistent.

Early, severe deprivation takes a toll on children's physical, cognitive, and social development. About one-half of the children first adopted from Romania scored in the range of retardation when their cognitive growth was examined at adoption. Lack of nurturing and stimulation contributed to their lack of skill mastery, and the longer the children were in an orphanage prior to adoption, the worse their outcomes. However, another amazing story of human resilience comes to light when we examine the Romanian adoptees. Famed British psychiatrist Michael Rutter found that by age four, those children who were adopted before six months of age had significantly higher cognitive functioning than their functioning at adoption. This group of children appeared to "catch up" with other children their age (see Rutter and O'Connor 2004). These data provide a snapshot of the power of enriched environments that include nurturing parents, even after beginning life with severe deprivation.

However, for those Romanian children who were adopted after age two, their scores on intelligence tests were lower at age six than that of British children who had not been institutionalized prior to adoption. Thus, length of time in an institutional environment with severe deprivation was a strong correlate of continued impairment. It appears that any prolonged severe deprivation of young children thwarts their normal development to a great extent. Their bonds with adults or lack of them were not enough to promote their growth. The importance of this social bond for cognitive development cannot be underestimated.

Attachment

Taken together, arguments for early nurturing and care for good Ph are supported. Children's cognitive development begins at birth and is critically dependent on adult caregivers' positive responses. The reciprocal bonds between caregivers and children are the foundation of the first learning environment. These early bonds of connection are often called "attachment" and simply mean that a set of behaviors develops between infants and their caregivers that are predictive of children's development. Those infants and caregivers who have a healthy psychological bond have interactions that promote a sense of comfort and readiness for the infant to explore his world.

By age six to eight months, these infant and caregiver interactions are evident. The infant looks to the caregiver as a "secure base" for exploration of his environment. The infant may explore various toys in his vicinity, but checking in with the primary caregiver or his secure base is evident at the same time. This role for the caregiver means that when separation of the infant and caregiver occurs, the infant very often signals distress by crying or whimpering. The caregiver may return to the child and offer soothing physical or verbal notes to the child: "It's OK. You play and Daddy will be right here." This interaction of two people engaged in psychologically healthy reciprocal processes helps calm the child so that he can return to whatever exploratory activity he was engaged in before their separation. The infant's ability to return to a previous activity is a marker of the strength and overall functioning of their social relationship, their attachment.

The construct of attachment is not without its critics, however. Primarily, predictions about future success that rely on attachment data have had mixed results. Some studies have found good links between early attachment categorizations and later outcomes, while others have not. Looking across cultures, children studied in Germany (Grossman and Grossman 1985) and Japan (Van Ijzendoorn and Kroonenberg 1988) appear to be dissimilar to children studied in the United States. From these studies, German children have more restraints from adults than do U.S. children, and Japanese children have more flexibility from adults than do U.S. children. These data tell a story of how attachment behaviors between infants and adults are related to cultural childrearing practices.

Other researchers have found the idea of one primary caregiver who promotes all growth, usually the mother, to be misogynist, racist, or misleading. For example, in the United States and among many African American families, multiple "primary" caregivers may exist. Siblings and other extended family members often have much responsibility for the care of young infants and the bonds these infants have with all of their caregivers can be characterized as healthy attachments (see Harkness and Super 1995). The traditional construct of attachment as a precursor to later development is not fully supported with psychological data. However, the concept of the importance of reciprocal interest and interactions between infants and their caregivers is found across ethnic groups and many cultures. The role of this interaction is to promote infant adaptation to new environments, whether in the home or elsewhere. These early bonds promote cognitive growth.

Exploring the Home and Relationships In It

From one year to two, the infant's world vastly expands. From the crib and loving arms to an entire apartment or house means a tremendous difference in an infant's environment. As the child moves about his surroundings by crawling, pulling up, and eventually walking, he sees possibilities for new discovery daily. Good Ph is developing simultaneously with cognitive growth.

Compliance and boundaries related to expectations of behavior help the young child to see how his behavior is related to others in a household. For safety and concerns about healthy development, adults may place physical boundaries on the "discovery zone." In this way, the infant begins to learn about a standard of behavior that is expected

by those who care about him. Along with boundary rules and prohibitions the infant is learning about compliance and consequences of
his behavior. For example, heating units in a home may pose a danger
to young children and caregivers must stick with a stated boundary
and prohibition. The caregiver's response should be precise and firm;
physical removal of the child near the unit to another area with equally
interesting toys is a form of discipline that concerns redirecting a
child, rather than punishing immediately. However, if the child continues to explore the heating unit, it is time for caregivers to take
other action.

"Time-out" is a tried and true remedy for young children's noncompliant behavior. Caregivers apply this consequence for the child's
behavior in different ways and, depending on the age of the child,
apply time limits that are appropriate. So, for our heating unit example, how does a caregiver employ time-out? A few simple rules will
help. Begin by considering the age of the child. For children from one
to two years, placing the child in an environment where locomotion
is limited can prove helpful; for example, the crib or playpen. Although
young children's command of language is limited, caregivers can make
a few short statements such as the following: "No, you cannot be on
the furnace. Stay in your crib for two minutes. You'll get another
chance to play." Make the timing obvious; use a timer with a bell or
buzzer. At the timer's signal, remove the child from the enclosure.
Place the child back to the safe area of the room that contains interesting objects he is allowed to play with. Caregivers may have to
repeat this action two or three times. If the child cannot self-regulate
and comply at this point, perhaps due to a lack of memory skill or
focus, it is time for another adult tactic. The concept of "baby proofing" a home is always advised in a proactive way.

Guards around a furnace or gates into the furnace room need to be
placed and their safety probability noted as well. Of course, caregivers must use common sense with safety prohibitions. Adults may take
little notice of children who are crawling on or playing around a heating unit when it is not in use during the warm months of the year. This
is ill-advised if the child must adhere to the safety rule in the winter
months. The lesson here in how to use time-out concerns the adult's
estimation of the child's self-regulation skills and a shift on the adult's
part if the time-out is too complex for the child to process cognitively.

By two years of age, this kind of short time-out will likely be effective with the child who has developed more compliance-ready behaviors. Alternately, any "baby proofing" of children's environments like that of electrical outlet covers, special locks on cabinet doors, or gate guards to rooms with unsafe conditions is always advised. Young children's safety in the home needs the same high priority commitment as stimulating their cognitive and social development. It is the responsibility of the adults in children's lives to attend to their desire for exploration and their safety.

While psychologists cannot be sure of infants' cognitive processing of compliance demands, we do know that rewards and punishments for behaviors are effective ways to change behavior in young children. For very young children, a short time-out in a crib or playpen with supervision can be an effective mode of behavior change. However, as always, rewards or praise for good behavior are more effective than punishment for noncompliant behavior. For example, when adults notice that a child has been playing well in a safe environment, making a concrete statement about this activity is a form of praise. "You are building with your blocks so nicely. I can get dinner done. Thank you." Caregivers' positive responses are welcome by infants and other young children. Standing ready to praise good behavior is a skill adults can master to help insure optimum development of children, including good Ph. When adults take time to develop a skill like praising good behavior, everyone benefits.

The use of time-out with young children teaches them that adults have rules for their safety and care and that there are consequences for their actions. While the development of self-regulation and compliance continues well into the adolescent years, early practice means that learning the rules of the home has begun. Children will need this early practice in order to be successful in other environments such as school and in order for whole families to operate smoothly.

The infant who begins exploring his world early with the support of important adults and older children is set for discovery. His early cognitive growth is marked and is that first solid stepping stone to toddlerhood. Learning about boundaries and consequences for behavior helps children learn personal responsibility and become important factors in a family's psychological health. With a few landmark mastery sets of language and locomotion developing, the early toddler years are fascinating to study as well.

From One Year to Two and Beyond

From one year of age to two, much cognitive development occurs as well. For example, the child's brain weight at age two is 75 percent of what his adult brain will become. Along with this developing brain size, more complex cognitions are progressing. Language development becomes quite rapid between one and two years. Words are attempted, including "holophrases" or words that stand for whole phrases. For example, "Up!" can mean "I want you to pick me up," or "Look up."

The first two years of children's cognitive development is extremely dependent on the good grace and good parenting of those around him. By the time the child is two, however, his manipulations of the environment include his own very skilled locomotion and curiosity in the world. With the cognitive growth accrued from birth to two, the child is well on his way to developing more cognitive skill over time. Just what can we expect for the cognitive development of children aged two to four? Expect thinking that is much more complex than that of an infant and yet not as developed as the child in the elementary-aged years. This hierarchy of development is fairly systematic and predictable.

From the ages of two to four the child's cognitive development remains quite evident. He can manipulate objects, increase a burgeoning vocabulary, and run freely in his environment. Cognitive growth during this period includes an increase in short-term memory skills, such as the ability to remember where last he left his toys or which toys bring him the most joy. His attention span is improving such that whole intricate play near others serves as a basis for cooperative play later with peers, older children, and adults. For example, at age two, stacking toy cups and saucers in a room with other children is an engrossing activity for the child. By age four that same child is interested in a tea party with a playmate.

The young child's perspective of the social world may still be egocentric in that it is difficult for him to understand the view or perspective of others. Yet, despite some of these limitations, young children are developing this skill. For example, a four-year-old child will speak differently to an infant than he does to another four year old. This kind of behavior tells us that this age child has some ability to shift with various social situations. He has some perspective that as people in his environment change, he must change also.

The two- to four-year-old child's coordination improves such that running is often a preferred mode of locomotion. Physically, entire homes and yards become the environments for cognitive discovery. Hand coordination means that he can dress himself with perhaps a little assistance early on, developing more skill as he reaches age four. All objects in his environment become potentially other learning opportunities for the child. Wheels are turned; wagons can be placed upside down for a tea party or a surface for a bouncing ball. Discovery is endless. Physical, cognitive, and social skills develop in concert as the child learns about his world. The child between two and four has mastered a lot of new information and is expected to operate with some independence from adults, albeit still within their supervision. Let us examine one great example of this interaction of physical, cognitive, and social development: the development of the child's control over his bladder and bowels. There are a few good guidelines for adults to consider about toilet training in general. Toilet training is another mastery skill set that has many developmental underpinnings before it can be used.

Parents often try to establish toilet training with their children early or before the children can master this skill. In the predominant culture of the United States, many adults spend a lot of time fretting about this particular skill set, but we do not have to do so. Both cognitively and physically, there is much that must be accomplished before adults should try to toilet train a child. The usual recommendation for toilet training is to try when the child is about 24 months of age. However, as always, this is not so for every child, so adults should temper the decision to begin with the knowledge that the list below provides. These guidelines can serve as a checklist for whether young children are ready for toilet training.

Toilet training and mastery
1 Is the child ready? Precursors such as the ability to understand directions and carry them out are necessary. Compliance to an adult request means that children can understand the request and act on it. If the child has not had similar adult demands like this previously, compliance may not occur. Children need practice with small compliance requests early in order to master the several skills needed for toilet training.

2 The young child's cognitive processing of noting information from his body, deciding what to do and acting is very complex for this age child, even with adult assistance.

3 Physically, the child's bladder may not be mature enough for the child to urinate four to five times daily in a toilet. If the urinating occurs more often than six times a day, his bladder is probably too immature for toilet training.

4 Hand coordination, dressing, and the ability to get to the bathroom all must be in place for the child.

5 Is the parent ready? Making a potty chair available is probably the easiest task for parents. Do so before beginning the training so the child has some curiosity and comfort with its presence in the home. Read to the child one or two books about toilet training as an accomplishment the child can master. Libraries and bookstores have these; read one to the child the day before beginning the training. If the child's curiosity about toilet training is piqued by the mere presence of the potty chair, by all means give it a try at that moment of interest on the part of the child.

6 Commit to a day with full attention and focus on the child. Be ready to encourage the child during the day and support the desired behavior when it occurs. Do not make the entire day "all about" toilet training, for this is just one part of being a young child.

7 Make the environment calm and free of tension. If adults can feel tension building, it is quite possible the child will as well. Remember that the child can accomplish this mastery skill set with adult assistance. Children often wish to please adults and mastery gives children a sense of accomplishment.

8 Make verbal suggestions positive. For example, when placing the "BIG GIRL" or "BIG BOY" training pants on the child, state "I bet you can pull these up." Assist the child if needed. Praise any approximation of success to this behavior.

9 Model sitting calmly for three to five minutes. Praise any effort the child makes to use the potty chair. "You're sitting still so you can listen to your body. That's great."

10 After a week or two, if tension builds because of the child's noncompliance, perhaps the child is not ready for toilet training. Give it a rest for one to two months before trying again. Practice smaller compliance demands on the child, such as putting away

toys or a cup. Praise any note the child gives you about urination or defecation. This shows he is considering his bodily functions. This by itself may constitute a new cognition for the child.

If the child is in care in another setting outside of the home, coordinated efforts with all other caregivers are needed. The cooperation of all adults and older children in the home will help make the teaching task easier. If the adults and older children in the home are comfortable with being a model for proper toilet behavior, allow the youngest child to observe this. Behaving in ways like that observed of older people, "like a grown-up," is often important for young children.

While toilet training is not solely reliant on cognitive skill, it is again one of those behavioral skill sets that children master because of increasing cognitive, physical, and social maturity at this age. Observing children's cognitive and physical readiness for this training makes adults better teachers. Any teacher can tell you that knowing their students is the best place to begin.

Readiness for Larger Learning Environments

Children from age four to six become skilled with the tools they need for kindergarten and elementary school. They are learning more about how to use language to make themselves understood; conversely, they are better able than the very young child to understand others. These children can hold a crayon or marker to create lines and figures and can very often tell others the story they have created to accompany the drawing. The children's focus is such that a *Sesame Street* program or even an entire children's movie can be attended to without a lot of movement. Children in this age group can follow the progression of a story whether on video or in a book. At this point, they may well recognize a few short words like "cat" or "dog" that are precursors to later reading, even prior to a preschool or kindergarten experience. The child who has been read to is the best predictor of those children who will become good readers themselves. Adults' interest in language and books is one of the first great models we provide to children as well.

By age five, rich discussions with this age child are likely. Many sentences strung together let adults know that the child's thinking is advancing rapidly. Whole paragraphs of dialogue stream forth and questions about the world and people in it seem endless. Memory for information and events is huge and they will absolutely correct any adult errors. For example, an adult who barks, "I told you to please stop that!" may have a child who states, "No, you did not. You did not say please."

Word play becomes a fun part of the children's developing vocabulary. Little "Knock, knock" jokes will delight and entertain this age child. "Knock, knock." "Who's there?" "Banana," said two times without resolution. On the third "Banana"-expected response, the response is instead "Orange." The child states "Who's there?" and the adult states "Orange you glad I didn't say banana!" Children at this age not only enjoy word play but they can generate it with some skill, too.

Look at this example of a four-year-old boy's word play. The child is strolling into an office building with his father. Along the way, he chants happily "I'm outside. I'm outside. I'm walking outside with Daddy." As the duo enters the building the boy begins to chant, "I'm inside, inside ..." until he spots a large atrium full of trees. The boy looks up at his father and chuckles. "The outside's inside!" Libraries and bookstores are chock full of books that promote word play. Read them with children to promote language skill development.

Children's self-control by age five usually includes focus over a period of time such that stimulation in the form of media or the manipulation of an object will hold their attention. This focus means that the child is learning to simply sit still as well. Do not underestimate the importance of this self-regulation in children's lives. A little practice with focus and stillness means that children's first years in a school setting will likely go smoothly. Whether adults ask children to read a book with them or sit still in other contexts, this practice is a great tool for the preparation of later formal teaching. Monitoring the child's comfort level yet increasing focused time will help the young child tremendously.

The "work" of children in the United States often concerns success in school. The child who is ready to focus when presented with new stimulation and possible mastery in the school environment has many new horizons opened up to him. Along with the benefits of cognitive development because of this focus, the child who is successful early in the classroom is very likely a socially adept child as well. Even young children wish to interact with other successful young children. At this age, this can be as simple as behaving in socially appropriate ways in the classroom. Listening to instructions, attempting to follow them, and staying in a chair are all examples of skills that show learning readiness in the young child.

Repetition and Modeling

Over the course of every child's development, adults are modeling behaviors that the child will repeat. This repetition of behaviors is a wonderfully adaptive mechanism. Yet what adult can honestly say that he is not worried about the repetition of some of his behaviors repeated by children? As humorous as this may seem, adults must keep this in mind as they go about their day around young children. Children's observational skills are quite good by the time the child is two to three years of age. If children see adults reading, exercising, working, playing, and maintaining caring relationships, these messages become powerful tools for the children's development. When young children repeat a motor activity they have seen adults engage in, like "stirring the pot" or jumping up and down because a favorite sports team scores on the television, adults remark about the wonder of this behavior. The children seem so small and cute as they mimic adult behavior! They are small and beautifully capable of repetition.

This adaptation to repetition means that adults have to carefully monitor their behavior around young children. Earlier in the chapter I wrote about the importance of reading to children and letting children observe others reading. Adults who wish to stimulate children's cognitive development should practice enjoying their own cognitive development as well. Lifelong learning is a goal many universities have for their college students now. Libraries and museums, art exhibits and music can be incorporated into families' weekly schedules as much as television and sporting events. All have their place in our cognitive development, but the stimulation of all our senses requires variety, alternatives for new discovery. When adults find joy in learning and in their own cognitive growth they provide a wonderful model for children to emulate.

Cognitive development over children's first five to six years is systematic and wonderful. I have presented the first measure for healthy

Ph as cognitive growth in the home, but the overlap of different forms of growth is evident. The social relationships adults have with children set them on a course for development with others outside of the home. The cognitive and social aspects of development operate in concert such that skill in one area often means skill in the other. We have taken a look at two mastery skill sets that require a neat coordination of physical, cognitive, and social skill in the child. The physically healthy child whose caregivers are in tune with his needs and attentive to provide enriched, stimulating environments for his cognitive growth has a solid building block for good Ph in the years to come. With early cognitive, physical, and social skill intact, the child is ready for cognitive growth outside of the home environment.

Chapter 3

Cognitive Growth Outside the Home

◆ ◆ ◆

The childcare teacher warmly greets a mom and motions for her to have a seat at the center. The mom sits quietly, looking expectant and hopeful that this first report about her child will be a positive one. The teacher begins their conference with an overall glowing report of the progress the three year old in question is making. Happy, active, works well with others. What a relief! The exact notes every parent wants to hear. Wait, there's something else? Yes, her focus is a bit less than that for completing one activity at a table. The teacher assures the mom that many three-year-old children need encouragement and practice with focus. The teacher explains how staff are working with the child to increase her focus and that they are already seeing some improvement. She is responding to their gentle encouragement. The mother asks how she can help. The teacher gives some pointers to the mom, a few ways to encourage the development of the child's focus from 10 to 15 minutes at home. As a last, positive note to the parent, the teacher says of the child with a smile, "She's my outside girl and my singing girl. She can play outside all day and when inside, she sings and hums with every task." The mom leaves with a cheerful heart.

This scenario was built around three positive points to consider. First, the childcare center staff meet regularly with parents for a short conference about the children. Second, teachers discuss strengths and opportunities for growth. Third, the parent is open to the teacher and responds in a collaborative way. These three facets of the scenario mean that the child's welfare and growth are the primary focus of the adults. When all adults responsible for children's development both inside and outside of the home work collaboratively, children's growth is facilitated.

My second measure for good Ph concerns a focus on the various environments in which children's cognitive growth is stimulated outside of the home. Children's cognitive growth occurs literally in every environment they are exposed to. In the United States, children experience a variety of care and cognitive stimulation. Early childhood beginnings include care by family members and others inside the home, as well as care outside of the home by private individuals or those who provide more formal childcare in an organization or center setting for a fee. Cognitive stimulation from phenomena like media enter children's lives daily as well.

As children grow, educational demands are placed upon them that mean several hours away from home in a school environment. This means that by ages five and six, most children in the United States are enrolled in a school program that is legislated or mandated by each state. Libraries, neighborhood centers, or recreational centers in urban and suburban areas are also places that provide after-school or summer learning opportunities for young children. Some rural areas offer this sort of after-school or summer center experience as well. These centers offer curriculum like reading, drawing, swimming etc. to young children and many offer quite elaborate curriculum in the summer months. Some religious organizations provide childcare and after-school and summer programs as well that include a combination of skill development and fun. Neighborhoods and communities provide other settings for learning in playground areas, sports programs, and organizations like Boy Scouts/Girl Scouts and the YMCA.

Some forms of cognitive stimulation that are generated outside of the home are pretty pervasive and enter the homes of the majority of Americans; media like television, movies, radio, and the Internet are such sources. All of these influences have the potential to stimulate children's positive cognitive growth. In this chapter I will focus on the factors that stimulate children's cognitive development in childcare and formal schooling, as well as media influences. Media are generated outside of the home but enter children's worlds every day, whether in the home or in other childcare and educational settings. We will look at parents as those adults most likely to make childcare and other educational experience decisions for children and how parents and teachers act as "filters" for the myriad influences upon children. Children need responsible adults to monitor and filter the many potential learning opportunities that can influence their growth; some may not prove growth-promoting to young children. Specific guidelines will be given concerning how to make responsible decisions about children's cognitive stimulation outside the home and how to be good filters in general. Adults in children's lives are responsible for filtering influences from the environment, with the hope that this early watchfulness will prove helpful to the children as they grow.

Recall that in chapter 2 we looked at how adults stimulate the early cognitive development of children by nurturing and caring for their overall wellbeing. These discussions centered on a child's development in the home environment over the first four years. In this chapter we will examine influences on children's cognitive growth external to the family environment and choices that responsible adults make concerning children's development from these influences.

Childcare Alternatives

Families in the United States have a range of possibilities for the care of their very young children prior to their entrance into a school environment. As the children grow, some possibilities emerge, like early childhood education through public or private preschool or prekindergarten programs. Following this, children then begin entry into private or public school environments for about twelve years. While the range of possibilities for early childcare is great, depending upon the circumstances of the family, not all options are available to every family. A look at the range of childcare options available is a good place to begin. Childcare possibilities include:

1   In the home with moms or dads.
2   In the home with other relatives or hired caregivers.
3   In a private home, formal agency, or childcare center, either part time such as a "Mother's Day Out" venue for a few hours a day or full time.
4   In neighborhood centers, religious institutions' day programming, youth sports teams, or community club facilities.
5   Any combination a family can muster!

Let's examine these possibilities. First, although more and more fathers are engaging in childcare now than thirty years ago in the United States, mothers still provide the majority of childcare for their children. Mothers are also more often the decision-makers concerning outside care and educational choices for their children. However, when all the adults responsible for children in the home contribute to these child-care and education choices, a commitment to being the best resources possible for young children is evident. When decisions like whether two parents should remain fully employed are considered, adults should have as their focus, "How can the best parenting occur?" Recall that parents are very powerful people in children's lives; their positive influence is seen in the children's Ph and outcomes as functional adults. Adults striving to best contribute to the development and good Ph of their children should be the focus of this decision-making.

Now, depending on your own position about maternal employment, early childhood, and childcare, these last few sentences can be interpreted to support any position. That is as it is meant, however. Any variation of childcare may work for one family but not for another. Each family decides which is best for them with a "best parenting possible" goal. For some families that include two parents, dual employment is a financial necessity that cannot be discounted. For others, maternal employment is a necessity for financial independence, adult development, or lifelong learning goals. For other families, maternal care in the home throughout the children's school years provides the best parenting for that household. Although this decision is not easily reducible to some checklist, adults in the home must weigh the factors they see as most important for the healthy growth of their entire family, while at the same time providing the best parenting possible to children. If a decision is made to seek external childcare, then attending to the options available and finding the most positive environment for children is necessary to insure their continued psychological and physical development.

Decisions about children's wellbeing and the adults' best parenting possible should be considered along with financial demands and other practical factors. Moreover, decisions like these are best discussed by adults when they are considering marriage partners, even prior to considerations about parenthood. The majority of women in the United States with young children work outside of the home, as do the majority of men. For adults who decide that some form of childcare is needed before the children are "school age" (five to six), there are guidelines supported by at least three decades of research in psychology for finding quality childcare and how best to use it as a positive support system to the family.

Childcare guidelines

1 Examine the child's resources. Consider her activity level and comfort with stimulation. Is her functioning around other infants and young children sufficient so that a large childcare setting seems feasible? Dependent on the age of the child, how gregarious is she? Would a small private home be a better fit?

2 Examine all of the childcare options. Complete this task before childcare is needed. Discuss options with other adults who have used various types of care. Seek referrals; network. Visit childcare centers and note the condition of the inside and outside environments. Interview potential childcare staff; seek letters of recommendation or those willing to be contacted. Seek caregivers who are licensed and can produce their license when asked. Check state licensing information by phone or Internet.

3 Determine the quality of care, including the number of children in the setting. Whether a licensed care facility in a private home or a large center, ratios of the number of children to childcare givers are set by state laws and usually range from 8–12 preschool children per one childcare staff member. The infant care ratio is usually smaller, 2–4 infants per one staff member. Ask staff for their center's ratio and make observations to corroborate that number. If the home or center operates at the peak ratio allowed, note whether the children are being tended to, whether they seem engaged and happy, whether the caregivers are calm and happy as well. Further, make this assessment with those centers with lower ratios. Visit at different times of the day. For example, examine how drop off and pick up times are handled by the staff; observe children's moods at the end of the day and how tired children are cared for by the staff. Request information about the staff's training and experience. While no childcare degree or certification guarantees a wise and caring teacher, both training and experience contribute to the success of childcare staff.

4 Examine the parents' resources. Financial considerations have to be worked out, but other factors should also be considered, for example lessening the number of hours children spend in care daily. In some studies, quantity of time spent in care is one factor that has been associated with negative child outcomes. However,

high-quality care often lessens or resolves other possible negative factors, including quantity of time spent in care. Families can make decisions to limit the amount of external care provided to children. For example, adults' schedules may be designed such that children can be in care for a 7-hour day, rather than a 9-hour day, if transport is collaboratively managed and adults' work hours have some flexibility. If children are raised in a two-parent family, involved fathers mean healthier child development in general, more family cohesiveness, less stress on women, and happier men.

5 Monitor the progress of children in any type of care. Have scheduled times for parent-teacher conferences and discuss developmental goals appropriate to the child's age. Discuss the various methods of cognitive, social, and physical stimulation and settings the childcare staff make available to children. For example, is drawing one part of the day or the entire day? Do the children spend a part of the day outside? If not, determine how the children's physical activity needs are met. What kind of food is served and how is it handled? These kinds of issues are also often controlled by state licensing boards that can be great information resources for adults. Happy, active children in quality care progress in cognitive and social skill development.

In sum, adults should examine childcare quality, time in care, and the type of care best suited for children and their families. Factors like father involvement and a supportive extended family are also a great part of the mix concerning childcare decisions and later developmental outcomes. These guidelines can help all families make good childcare decisions, provided they have the financial means to examine all options and choose the highest quality childcare in the region. For more details and helpful information related to childcare decisions, see the notes and websites at the end of this chapter.

Maternal Employment Debate

Maternal employment is often debated in public ways that appears as a sort of game about who is to blame for children who are at risk for a variety of poor outcomes. Notice that no attention is given to fathers' employment status as these debates ring out. In reality, there is no "right" way for families to rear their children except for the "best parenting possible" consideration. Adults who are actively involved with children are needed for good Ph outcomes.

Do children at home with exclusive maternal care differ in important ways from children who attend childcare or non-maternal care? This is a complicated issue because of the extent to which other important factors vary with the use of childcare. For example, families with educated adults who use childcare centers have better parenting skills than families who opt for exclusive maternal care. It is likely that the more educated the adults are in a family, the more likely they will know about good parenting, either through their own educational backgrounds or through the childcare workers who teach them skills. Perhaps lower-income families more often choose to care for their children in the home because of a lack of funds to seek external care. Education and income are two of the factors that are not well understood, as they vary together. The shortest answer is that children in formal childcare have greater cognitive and social stimulation and are more school-ready than children who are raised solely in maternal care (see Network 2006).

However, a few studies have revealed a finding of greater negative social behavior among children in childcare, compared to children raised solely in the home (Network 2006). Logically, this is not too surprising. A diverse group of children are often together in childcare, at least diverse in the sense of family backgrounds and rules for behavior. Toys and other stimulating objects are community property and playtime often means learning negotiation skills. The number of children playing together in formal care often provides more opportunities for disagreement than for those children in maternal care. Both formal childcare and exclusive maternal care have value for families. However, the debate about maternal employment is nonsensical, since most families need childcare in the United States. We should be debating how to best support families in general, promote the best parenting possible, and act upon our available research.

Childcare and Early Education
Needs in the United States

Former president of the American Psychological Association (APA), Diane F. Halpern initiated a task force in 2004 within the APA to examine the research evidence concerning work-family interface and its impact on American families (see Halpern 2005). The task force found that changing demographics and cultural/social change meant that within a three-generational period of time, early 21st century families' everyday lives were very different from those who came before. More women were employed and more children were in childcare than in 1950. In the majority of families in the United States at the dawn of the 21st century, employed mothers with children in childcare is the prevailing reality. The task force found two important facts that are particularly relevant to this discussion of the interface of parental employment, childcare, and the cognitive outcomes of children. Simply put, the APA task force overwhelmingly agreed that poverty is the factor most detrimental to children's cognitive development. They also stated that employed parents are not at all detrimental to children's outcomes, but found that the lack of childcare options for families is a formidable problem. Further, most childcare options are not available for families who must choose childcare based solely on low cost.

The "working poor" or those families who have one or two adults with two or more low-paying jobs do not have many options for childcare. Nor do these families qualify for government-subsidized childcare. Low-income families often must rely on low-quality childcare; overworked and stressed teachers, not enough stimulation for the children in care, etc. Outcomes for children in low-quality care are compromised. The United States is the only Western industrialized country without subsidized childcare for all and without legislated paid maternal/paternal leave upon the birth of children. Childcare in the United States is an issue that many psychologists state is the major dilemma facing families and our society in general.

Mother-only households comprise a large proportion of the low-income families who have few childcare options. What of the cognitive development of those children being raised in mother-only households? Although their outcomes vary just as children from other family configurations, their development is often compromised. Let us look at these children so as to understand the interface of employed work, families, and public policy.

In the United States approximately 33 percent of all children are being raised in a single-parent household, 95 percent of whom are mothers (Halpern 2005). Of these children, the majority has no involvement nor income provided to them by their fathers; most live in poverty. Poverty environments thwart children's cognitive development and put them at high risk for later school drop out and criminal behavior. When the single mothers who once received federal and state funds attempt to leave government assistance, their employment capabilities and histories are such that they are often relegated to the poorest-paying jobs, often without health insurance or childcare assistance. They become, euphemistically, part of the working poor. Add to this picture a lack of childcare options, especially when children are ill, and we see women returning to government assistance at a high rate. However, one childcare program that has had a good success rate with the cognitive and social stimulation of poor children is Project Head Start.

Project Head Start is an enriched environment that provides free childcare to poor families, often headed by single mothers, who can qualify. The federal government funds these programs in low-income neighborhoods. While not all Head Start centers are of high quality, those that are provide much needed care and educational readiness skills to low-income children. When young children can enter kindergarten with cognitive skills (e.g., letter and number recognition) and social skills (e.g., taking turns and staying in a chair for short periods of time), the children's cognitive outcomes are positive. These children are more likely to finish high school, delay marriage and pregnancy, avoid criminal behavior, and have overall higher functioning than those children who lack these skills when they begin formal schooling (Halpern 2005). Such enriched, stimulating environments for children from ages two to five are often termed "early childhood education" (ECE). When children are around four years of age, these environments are often called "preschool" or "pre-kindergarten (pre-K)."

ECE centers cannot be distinguished from some childcare centers and are often just a more structured continuation of skills learned in the same childcare setting for children aged one to two. For the healthy development of children's cognitive skill, ECE and preschool centers make substantial contributions to families. For families who can afford quality ECE, the benefits are undeniable. However, children in poverty, including those in the category of the working poor, often must rely on other relatives for care or upon childcare of poor quality. The renowned economist J. J. Heckman has said that the responsibility of society is to promote the welfare of all of its human capital, and that quality preschool access for all is the best way to promote this human capital. This Nobel Prize-winning economist sees the human capital potential to society when children's development is supported (see Carneiro and Heckman 2003). Look at these data reported in 2003 by the U.S. Department of Education:

> High quality, educational childcare and preschool for low-income children by age 15 reduces special education placements and grade retentions by 50 percent compared to controls; by age 21, more than doubles the proportion attending 4-year college and reduces the percentage of teenage parents by 44 percent. (Dynarski et al. 2003: iii)

The cognitive development of children is inextricably related to their futures and to their progeny's future. The external environments of childcare and early childhood education are powerful contributors to the overall health of children. Adults responsible for children's good Ph must weigh all factors when making decisions about childcare and other factors that strengthen families with the goal of providing the best parenting possible. Whether or not children have had good preparation for formal schooling, all must attend such schooling as mandated by state legislatures in the United States.

Let's now turn to the formal school environment's impact on children and families.

"Elementary, my dear Watson"

When Sherlock Holmes explained his expert powers of deduction to his friend Dr. Watson he did so with the phrase that serves as a heading to this section. Holmes meant by this that his deductions were simple, easily understood, readily grasped. Such is the definition of "elementary" in our dictionaries. While we would all hope that the elementary school years mean an accumulation of skills that are easily grasped by all children, we know that not every child will find this to be so. However, adults in children's lives are responsible for finding the best possible match for children's school readiness, school experience, and outcomes in general.

Good cognitive and social stimulation in the home and in childcare provides many building blocks for later development in children. Those children with solid backgrounds in early childhood education skills will achieve in school. Children who are ready to tackle reading and number manipulations with focus and socially appropriate behavior are the classroom stars. Unfortunately, our society's commitment to developing these school-ready skills is lagging compared to the need, as evidenced by the lack of preschool availability in the United States. This lack of a coherent public policy means that not all children will fare well when formal schooling begins. Elementary school staff who are charged with educating young children are often the first adults to build a foundation for these children's cognitive development; the children without preschool experiences begin school under a cloud of deficit.

The neighborhood public school has been under much criticism from many fronts over the last twenty years. Politicians are divided concerning how to strengthen public schools in the United States, with some calling for more financial support and others calling for voucher systems to allow children in poor school districts to attend a school of their family's choice, including private schools. While this debate continues, children in the United States are being short-changed, their development not supported by the adults responsible for their outcomes. Psychologists and educators have the data that show how to support children and schools. When these disciplines and the state and federal governments decide to work together, progress can be made. Moreover, schools that succeed despite the limitations placed upon them by society do exist in the United States.

The Effective School Ethos

In the United States it is believed that all children deserve an education as a basic right. We legislate education, but often give lip-service only to equal access to quality educational environments. We provide education in all of the fifty states, but at varying rates of quality and success. Psychiatrist and Yale University professor James Comer has examined urban schools and has developed a school ethos of collaborative planning that includes all stakeholders. These ideas are supported with years of research about how to strengthen schools in general. Look at some of Comer's core ideas:

1 Focus on child development. Adults responsible for children's education must know the skills necessary for their development, both physical and psychological.

2 Focus on school staff development. Well-trained, collaborative administrators, teachers, and counselors provide the best environments for children.
3 Focus on community development. Bridge school staff, parents, and community members (e.g., librarians, childcare workers, etc.) so that all groups are empowered to work together for effective schools.
4 A commitment by all adult stakeholders facilitates responsible, goal-driven behavior in children. (Check this chapter's endnotes for questions to consider as school choices are evaluated.)

What Comer (2004) proposes reflects the concept of adult responsibility to children already discussed. He is also a very strong proponent of the necessity of relationship-building between these responsible adults. When children's developmental needs are addressed by educators, in collaboration with parents and other adults in a community, children's growth is promoted. Children see this commitment and empowering collaboration by adults and respond with their own positive behaviors. This is the public school that all adults in the United States want for their children. It is achievable and within reach. In fact, Comer's ideas have been implemented in over 600 schools in the United States, with positive results.

When responsible adults set high standards for themselves and their children, with accountability measures for both the adults and children, our children win. This is not to say that "simple" solutions to school reform like standardized testing are the answer – quite the contrary. Personal and public accountability can be accomplished by measuring signs of growth in each child, with an emphasis on keeping children in school by means of teaching them the beauty of life-long learning and its rewards. Good collaborative efforts by all responsible adults promote positive relationships between teachers and children in the classroom. Teachers who feel they have been well educated and well supported in their efforts to provide a learning environment based on collaborative relationships are successful. All of the children in these teachers' classrooms can succeed and with the passing of each school year become better thinkers and informed citizens themselves.

Undoubtedly, a question may arise about the intellectual capability of all students for school success, even in an "effective school." Critics of this egalitarian approach will say that not all children can learn.

While we know that some children may begin school with intellects that may be in the range of retardation, this is not the case for the majority of our youth in the United States. More often, we have groups of children who are characterized as not teachable because of a lack of school-ready behaviors and bias. Whether ingrained or unintended, this bias has a great impact on thousands of children. Standards of excellence for all children and a concept known as "stereotype threat" have been researched by two stellar social psychologists in the United States, Claude Steele and Joshua Aronson (1995). Both are experts in the area of expectation and performance.

Schooling and Stereotype Threat

In the 1990s, Claude Steele and his colleagues began studying groups of students who were not performing well in class, yet who had high intellectual capacity. Steele focused his early work on female students who were attempting to enter previously male-dominated fields like engineering and black students who were attending highly competitive universities. He found that when students felt a threat of being stereotyped as people who were not skilled enough to enter new environments, the students failed or withdrew to salvage part of their self-esteem. Such stereotype threats were pervasive.

One example that is particularly relevant to this discussion concerned the practice at one large university of offering their entering black freshmen class remedial course work as part of their orientation to the college. This kind of expectation is the opposite of James Comer's advice concerning communicating high standards to all students and supporting them in their efforts. These entering freshmen had high marks on standardized tests in high school and had already performed admirably prior to entering the university. Steele went on to offer sage advice based on his research.

If the goal of education is to promote learning for all, then separating some students from others is not helpful. Such exclusion serves to promote stereotyping of these students. If some freshmen entering college have transitional difficulties that need ameliorating, then offer "strength training" or "transitional assistance" to all entering freshmen. In this way, all students can choose to avail themselves to this curriculum and no one group of students is characterized as needy of remediation. Joshua Aronson (2002) applied these findings to elementary and secondary schools and the amelioration of stereotype threat in these settings as well.

Communicating a high expectation of success for all is one facet of classroom learning that is an absolute necessity in education, according to Joshua Aronson. Like James Comer and Claude Steele, Aronson believes this standard is developed and transmitted through good social relationships between teachers and students. Cognitive development is a social endeavor and intellect itself is highly malleable. Collaborative adults can create meaningful pathways by which all students can develop cognitively and have school success. However, when distrust, stereotyping, and exclusionary practices are evident in the classroom, children cannot learn. Adults' expectations, whether positive or negative, are communicated to children and they respond in a reciprocal way or withdraw completely.

Ameliorating Bias

Cognitive development and academic achievement are promoted for all students when adults interested in successful schools focus upon various psychological factors. Factors like intellect, self-esteem, inclusion, and decreasing bias all contribute to the cognitive outcomes of children in the school environment and thus promote good Ph. How to design and implement an effective school has been set forth by experts like James Comer, yet many of our schools in the United States struggle to offer unbiased, inclusive instruction. For example, a higher percentage of ethnic minority children fail to finish high school than Caucasian children (Santrock 2007). While many factors, including poverty, contribute to this outcome, our schools can be a structured haven where all children thrive. Ethnic minority children will remain in school if relationships have been fostered between them and all relevant adults who wish them to be successful.

Diversity of background and experience is increasing among the ranks of teachers in the United States, yet the majority remains Caucasian. The majority of all teachers are committed to help all children develop strong cognitive and social skills and wish to do so without bias. Teachers of all backgrounds need training in multiculturalism for their own professional development that will translate to school success for children. Such multicultural training is available in the sense that this kind of curriculum exists, yet not many school districts train their staff both top-down and bottom-up to be able to use the training effectively. Administrators must exhibit the same multicultural sense that they expect of their teachers. Teachers' own worldviews must include the expectation that all students possess aptitudes for learning when they reach the school environment. Whole communities must commit to work together to strengthen schools. After- school supervision and stimulation through libraries and other entities with a child focus are needed to help insure that students who may have lacked early childhood education are not lost to the negative influences that abound. How to reach every student should be the goal of whole communities. As Aronson has stated, cognitive growth is reliant on social relationships and is highly malleable. Schools in collaboration with other adults in a community can stimulate positive cognitive growth in all children, where inclusion and egalitarian beliefs are promoted. This is the real essence of school reform.

Ready for the Next Step

Children in their early years of schooling learn complex skills over a fairly short period of time. Their elementary years are usually just six to seven years of their lives, yet their cognitive development shifts from simple recognition of letters and numbers to their manipulation to make sense of the world. By the time the children reach third grade they are capable of complex thought like reading and solving number equations. By around age eleven or twelve, these same children are ready to tackle ever more complex manipulations of words and numbers that include "abstraction" and "meta-cognition." Abstract thought means thinking with words and numbers hypothetically, even into the future, and meta-cognition refers to thinking about thinking. Whew! Two examples will assist in the understanding of these terms.

When a child examines a math problem, she thinks about the possible manipulations necessary to solve the equation. As she develops, she can consider some manipulations without physically putting these on her paper. She will likely consider several options for solving the problem and select one. This is an example of abstract thought. This same child may begin to solve the math problem but get frustrated. After a few minutes, she may say to herself, "I've done these problems before without much difficulty. I'm really taking a long time trying to solve this one. I wonder if there's some reason I'm not focusing or if I'm just thinking about this one too much." She is examining her own problem-solving, or thinking about thinking. Her meta-cognition will likely help her decide what to do next. The rudiments of these skills are new to the child leaving elementary school. As she enters the broader middle school setting, such skills will continue to develop.

Middle School

When children are ready to enter middle school, also termed "junior high school," their nascent ability to use abstract thought helps them to focus on more than one problem and solution at a time. This increased ability also helps their social relationships. For example, they become more capable of considering another's perspective. By age twelve, these qualitative changes to children's memory have begun and along with it, new skills to help them organize and memorize information. Greater memory skills and the ability to see two sides of an issue also mean that children's critical thinking is developing. While these skills are not as developed as they will be when the children leave their high schools, the beginnings of these new skills are evident.

At around age twelve children are expected to have greater independence from teachers and parents concerning their cognitive growth than that expected of them during the elementary school years. Middle school teachers assign more independent study in the form of homework or projects they expect to be completed in the home environment for a grade at school. As usual, those children reared in supportive home environments often succeed in school. The interface between adults who are school staff and parents is one of the most important aspects of adults' responsibility to children during these years. School staff members who seek parental collaboration have more successful students. While these qualities may be evident in an elementary school setting, they remain important as children develop during their adolescent years.

Adult caregivers who find child-friendly, family-friendly teachers and administrators in an elementary school should look for the same collaborative ethos and interest in middle school and high school staff. Children transitioning to their middle school years have some complex issues to handle and continue to need adult collaborations for their success. One of the contributing factors to this complexity is the physical growth of children and pubertal changes that affect cognitive development.

Biological and Environmental Transitions

In the United States we ask children to move into new school environments at the same time their bodies are transitioning into reproductive capability. From elementary to middle school, children are expected to make several big changes quickly. As noted above, more is expected of the children concerning greater autonomy for their own learning. The middle school environment is usually larger and has many more students than the elementary school; therefore, more is expected of the children concerning social relationships. Children often must learn how to work with 7–8 teachers a day instead of the usual 2–3 teachers found in elementary school. These class changes also mean that peer relationship configurations likely vary from one hour of the day to the next. New modes of thinking and many new people have to be processed and integrated into the child's repertoire of knowledge in order to be successful in middle school. Top this off with an increase in pituitary and hormone activity and what have we concocted? A recipe for a tough transition period for many children. Fortunately, the majority of children cope with all of these changes with the help of collaborative adults.

Physical changes mean new questions for children around age twelve. They may feel clumsy or even ugly as their physical development progresses. They consider how changes in their appearance affect their relationships; whether others will find them attractive and pleasant to be around. Such questions are rarely considered by young children, as their thinking about the perspectives of others is limited. The child entering early adolescence has a much more complex world to consider. Changes in their bodies, changes in expectations, and changes in environments can occur seemingly overnight.

Happily, most children survive these changes that can contribute to poor outcomes, their vulnerability changed to success through their own stamina and skill and the support of teachers and parents. Peers are also a very important part of this equation (we will focus on this in chapter 5). In fact, the amount of media attention given to vulnerable children who do not succeed and have poor outcomes is misleading. Most children survive and thrive in their adolescent years with the help of supportive adults. How did we come to emphasize the poor outcomes of approximately 15 percent of our youth? Several factors contribute to this emphasis. Recall that psychology as a discipline first sought to ameliorate social ills, including poor outcomes for children. This is laudable, yet we failed to examine resilient children for decades. Media often report children's poor outcomes as newsworthy or eye-catching. After all, the role of news media is to inform us about all kinds of news. Perhaps psychologists have failed to inform the public that most children succeed in school and are not breaking the law. Whatever contributed to the public's understanding of adolescents, we have not told their stories well.

When adults generalize the poor outcomes of a few highly visible adolescents in the media to all adolescents, we not only short-change the vast majority of adolescents who do thrive, but we also devalue the adolescents who need collaborative, supportive adults the most. We often depict the adolescents who are struggling as innately flawed. Here is a newsflash I would like everyone to memorize: None of our sons are "natural born killers," none of our daughters are innately selfish pop princesses. Our children become the people who we socialize. Adults responsible for adolescents can take heart that years of facilitating cognitive and social growth in children will not be in vain. Early lessons learned are not forgotten, although as every parent or teacher of adolescents can attest, some important lessons have to be uncovered from time to time in our interactions with them. Children need positive stimulation and collaborative adults who care about them. One neat intersection of school and home that has been proven effective for good cognitive outcomes is extracurricular activities.

Extra! Extra! Extracurricular!

Although obvious to school personnel for decades, we now have data that show the activities associated with non-academic time at school are predictive of academic success for children (Gilman, Meyers, and Perez 2004). Children who are engaged in activities like fine arts or athletics perform better cognitively than their unengaged peers.

Further, even "club" activities offered like Math, Foreign Language, or Chess Club contribute these same benefits. What is going on? Why would children who spend more time at school have greater success in general? Various indicators of how extracurricular activities contribute to positive outcomes emerge and are not surprising, given findings from psychological research.

Children who commit to extracurricular activities do so because of a variety of reasons. What promotes this interest?

1   Parents want their children to develop as fully as possible.
2   Employed parents need care for their children before or after school.
3   School staff members want students to develop as fully as possible.
4   School staff members' success contributes to their career and schools' success. A happy, thriving school band or ball team helps teachers' careers and promotes school pride for teachers and students.
5   Children enjoy being with their peers.
6   Children benefit from developing relationships with teachers outside of the classroom.
7   Some children flourish with physical activity, the beauty of fine arts, or competition in general.
8   Adults collaborate for extracurricular program success.
9   Children see adults' collaboration as a model for collaborative behavior with their peers and with adults.
10 Whole communities are strengthened by successful schools.

The ideas listed are those that promote children's interest in extracurricular activities. The underpinnings of these make sense. While not all children will develop an extracurricular skill to the extent that professional musicianship or ball playing is an outcome, the sheer enjoyment of relationship-building and learning about the self in supportive environments that are "extra" to the classroom experience are valuable. We see responsible adults working together to promote the overall development of children, including their good Ph. Children are empowered and positive outcomes are correlates of these activities.

However, some children do not have extracurricular opportunities and not all who do have positive experiences. Adults responsible for children should be watchful of these possibilities, as well.

Not all children have families who can support their interests financially in extracurricular activities. Musical instruments can be expensive; transportation to and from school can be difficult, etc. Adults who are responsible for children must consider how to support all children's engagement in the life of the school outside of the classroom as well as inside. So, for those expensive musical instruments, consider how schools can make used instruments available to those children without the economic means to buy them. Not all school districts budget for this sort of support, but many do. School districts are often devoid of transportation assistance to children in extracurricular activities; their tight budgets do not cover these "extras." These challenges constitute another opportunity for all adults to work together to tackle problems associated with children's extracurricular participation. Parents, teachers, and other community partners can come together to brainstorm ideas for ameliorating barriers to extracurricular activities, including neighbors helping neighbors with car pools, etc., to help children experience an array of cognitive, social, and physical stimulation.

Some children who are fortunate enough to participate in extracurricular activities do not have positive experiences. Some are "pigeon-holed" to excel in activities they are not interested in because of prior family success in one area (e.g., dad's an accomplished pianist, mom's an award winning basketball player, etc.). Other children are expected to engage in too many activities at once, which can leave them exhausted. While "over-involvement" in extracurricular activities is not well researched, common sense and monitoring children's scholastic achievement, energy, and interest levels should help adults consider what amount of these activities promote the children's overall development. Children can also participate in extracurricular peer groups that are at risk for alcohol or other substance abuse (Endresen and Olweus 2005). If an extracurricular group has a reputation at the school for risky behavior, adults who monitor children should be aware of this and take steps to ameliorate the problem. Peer group influences can be positive or negative, as we will examine further in chapter 5.

Adults who do support children's extracurricular activities must be watchful that all children are given a chance to participate, that their efforts are recognized and valued and their general development encouraged. Relationship-building occurs when children work toward a common goal as a team. These are just a few notes for adults to consider when assessing the extracurricular programs that are available. For example, whether fine arts ensembles or whole ball teams, how is each child's participation handled? Do the adults responsible for the programs have good Ph outcomes in mind as they teach or coach? How are disappointments handled? A low score for an orchestra competition or team loss on the field presents teaching and learning moments for children. How responsible adults handle these travails not only serve as models for children's behavior, but can contribute to the children's overall Ph as well. When all adults responsible for children are watchful that other positive growth occurs along with this extracurricular skill development, children's growth is promoted. Often, the skills associated with extracurricular activities in middle school can be transferred to the high school environment. They can serve as a transitional pathway for children entering yet another larger environment in many school districts. Peer relationships forged in extracurricular activities are often maintained and assist with the transition to high school as well.

High School

The cognitive development of children in high school differs a great deal from their early years of schooling in elementary schools. In the United States many high schools are quite large and resemble small college campuses. Literally, these schools are called "campus-style high schools," indicating their large geographic and student population size. While not all city or suburban schools have large high schools, many do. This is another assessment those adults responsible for children must engage in as they consider where to live and how to provide optimal school experiences for children. For example, if large, suburban districts recognize that their student population is huge, how do they help students achieve cognitive mastery and build relationships in such a setting?

Strategies like "teacher teams" or "small learning communities" are currently gaining popularity in the United States. Teachers who communicate across their discipline domains can get to know groups of students who are assigned to them; for example, a student's math teacher can find the same student's science teacher to compare notes about how to best stimulate or manage a child. When teachers can act as a coherent team, large high schools can contribute positively to children's cognitive and social development.

"Small learning communities" is a phrase that refers to the students' ability to choose an area of interest and experiment in this area for a year or more in high school. School staff usually define the communities or choices offered to students. For example, students who are interested in medicine as a possible career would choose an associated learning community. Ostensibly, students who choose a particular learning community track would share interests, be supportive of each other, and have teachers with great interest in the specific areas as well. Teachers within these learning communities design curriculum around the interests of their students and themselves. For example, most high schools require students to take several science courses that will accrue as credits toward graduation. The students who choose medicine as their learning community would likely be advised to take one science course like Anatomy and Physiology over Introduction to Computer Engineering. Such strategies as teaching teams or small learning communities have been proven effective for school personnel to promote the cognitive development of large numbers of students.

As adults decide how to support children in various high school environments, a commitment to relationship-building and high expectations for all children will assist our children in their late adolescent years. Children with good Ph can move from the home environment into the broader contexts of employed work or college with a solid foundation. Cognitive development outside of the home will continue as the children move into adulthood.

The title of this chapter denotes a child's learning in environments outside of the home. However, as promised, I also wish to examine one influence on children that is generated outside of the home, yet enters our homes, schools, childcare facilities, and workplaces with regularity: the media.

Media, Children, and Adult Filters

Media are any public forms of communication that seek to inform or entertain. Thus, media can be print, video, or audio. Media influences can be positive, negative, inconsequential, or perversely pervasive. Adults responsible for children can serve as good filters of this influence so that children's good Ph is promoted. One example that is quite pervasive in the United States is television programming.

By the late 1960s, television aimed at children in the United States came under scrutiny when a handful of activist adults decided to monitor what was being shown to children and to advocate for more learning opportunities in television programming. *Sesame Street* and "children's television" was born. Not many American children in the 21st century can say they do not know Kermit, Ms. Piggy, Big Bird, Elmo, and Ernie. The characters peopled by actors on the show and the puppets revolutionized children's programming. Stories about reading, numbers, or being a friend were portrayed with nurturing care along with big doses of humor delivered through words, visual art, music, and dance. While we can look to *Sesame Street* as the forerunner of our modern *Dora the Explorer* or *Blue's Clues*, the majority of television programming today is still not made for the education or the consumption of children. Those richly textured shows that do educate children remain in the minority and are more often in venues like public television, rather than for-profit television, movies, and the like. Educational and entertainment programming for children has increased over the last two decades such that a few entire networks now focus on children. This is good news for the children and the adults who care about them. However, adult filters are still needed with the majority of media influences that bombard the public (Smith and Donnerstein 1998).

Adults who filter media influences to children are doing the whole of society a great favor. Even media executives will say that what they produce is not always suitable for children and that it is up to adults in children's lives to monitor media programming. Neither the television, nor the video player, nor the computer is a good childcare provider; adults who monitor and filter all media for children in their care are. All media forms can be used to promote the growth of children and their good Ph. Several avenues exist to assist adults who monitor and act concerning media influences.

Adult filters of media
1 Use age-appropriate media for educational and entertainment activities in moderation.

2 Be constantly mindful of what media are available when children are present, no matter what the environment. Pay attention to the content; question whether it is a good influence. Discuss with the children present.
3 Change the media output that is objectionable or inappropriate for the age child who is consuming it or remove the child from the environment.
4 Explain the change of media behavior. If the media already occurred and the images or sounds were disturbing to the child, discuss this. For example, if a preschool child is exposed to violent images on a TV program, make statements that reflect the child's response to the images and what meaning can be made of the images. State: "That's upsetting and sad to me. Want to talk about it? People must learn to work together for the good of all. Let's watch something that shows how to get along." Depending on the age of the child, this dialogue may not be possible. However, adults can structure their responses appropriate to the programming and the cognitive skill of the child.
5 Model being an informed consumer. Adults who select appropriate media stimulation give children a model for their own behavior, a permission to become their own filters. By age three to four, if a child can make a statement like "That scares me, turn it off," the adults have done a good job.

These few tips can be very helpful as adults try to filter media influences. Similar situations may arise with computers, movies, and even newspapers or books children pick up to read. Adults who give children information about the influence of media can help the children be mindful of the values those adults espouse. Should neighbors, relatives, or public places show media that are inappropriate for children, be empowered to say, "This is not good for this child." While none of us can control other adults, speaking the values we espouse allows the children we are responsible for to hear our commitment and see that we act on it. This means that, yes, neighbors may allow their three year olds to watch R-rated movies or MTV. However, adults who advocate for children and responsible media programming transmit their values to the children in their care. These values often prevail with children as they grow.

Just what is in the media that adults may want to filter? Violence, homophobia, racism, sexism, and explicit sexual content in the media are areas of concern for responsible adults. Good judgment about children's developmental level may help adults filter media content sufficiently, but a look at violence and sexual content in the media will shed some light on media concerns in general.

Debates about violence in the media and its effects on children have occurred for about the last thirty years. Presidential commissions, as well as researchers in psychology and other disciplines, have attempted to examine the issue. We have several decades of research that shows media violence is a negative factor in children's lives. According to two psychologists specializing in media violence, Stacy L. Smith and Edward Donnerstein (1998), media violence is related to children's negative behaviors, but the parameters of that relationship are not yet truly understood. Psychologists are studying how media violence is related to aggression in children. Several factors have been found that are linked with aggressive responses in children. For example, more aggressive responses are found if the victim of violence is not portrayed as suffering, and if the perpetrators are attractive and do not experience the consequences of their actions. In other words, attractive, violent "heroes" to whom no negative consequences occur and whose victims are portrayed as irrelevant are the "best" models for promoting aggression in children. Television, film, and videogame violence is believed by organizations like the American Psychological Association and the American Medical Association to be a contributor to violence in the United States. Indeed, the Centers for Disease Control view media violence as a contributor to a national epidemic of juvenile violence in the United States. The amount and depth of violence in the media is greater today than twenty years ago and children need adults who act responsibly. The data detailed above should assist adults who wish to monitor and filter such influences.

Sexual content in the media is another area of concern for responsible adults. With sexual content, however, very little longitudinal data exist that show a relationship between the content and children's behavior over time. One very recent study by Steven Martino[16] and his colleagues at the Rand Institute was published in the journal *Pediatrics* (Martino et al. 2006). They found that listening to music lyrics that referred to degrading sexual experiences like female victimization and male abuse was significantly related to adolescents' first intercourse and non-coital sex. The more degrading sexual messages the adolescents heard, the earlier they were engaging in sex themselves. Sexual content in the media can be accessed by children as easily as turning on a radio, a computer, or television at any time of the day.

Throughout much of the 1980s, television networks adhered to a code of self-censorship, and programs with sexual content were shown after 9 or 10 p.m. so that adults could filter this content for children. No more. With cable networks and Internet access to pornography and irresponsible sexual behavior, children are now consumers of this kind of media. Within this content several patterns emerge.

Adolescents and adults are often portrayed on television as highly sexualized in their behavior without relational commitment. Whole stories or features revolve around each character's sex partners. Rarely are models depicted such that sexually active people have dialogue about responsible sex or birth control, or have consequences for irresponsible sexual behavior. In a summary article in the *Journal of Sex Research* about media influences on adolescent sexuality, Jane D. Brown reported findings from several studies that show adolescents are using media for information about sex and as models for their own sexual behavior (Brown 2002). For example, adolescents reported a higher acceptance of non-marital sexual behavior as their exposure to sexual content in the media rose. More exposure to sexually explicit images is related to adolescents' estimates of unusual sexual activity (e.g., group sex, bestiality, and less commitment to one partner). Sexually explicit movies also contribute to young people's callous views about rape, as though this act of criminal assault is not so bad because of its depiction as a part of "nonconsensual sex," without bloody aggression and no bad outcomes for the victim. Children need adults who assert that nonconsensual sex is rape; it is a crime. Correlational studies have found a relationship between exposure to sexual content on television and first intercourse among adolescents. That is, the more sexual content the children watch, the earlier their first intercourse (Brown 2002).

Risk-free sexual expression is not a reality. While sexuality is a normal part of development and an important part of people's lives, responsible adult messages about commitment and risk are needed. These are rarely found in the media. Because risk-free sexual expression is such an ever-present message in the media, it behooves responsible adults to talk with children about sexual behavior as normal, beautiful, and a part of people's commitment to one another as we develop.

One last note of caution concerns the availability of computer social networks that are so popular with children of all ages currently. While adults may not be aware of violence or sexual content in these social networks, both have been found. Children post violent and sexual images and verbal content on their social network spaces. Adults posing as children are doing the same. Parents and teachers who monitor and filter media content for the children in their care should also be cognizant of the computer as another source of possible negative influence. In general, adults who are not as computer literate as their children should get advice from others who are; learn how to check children's computer use. Children's interactions on the computer social networks can be explicitly monitored and the children should be told the adults are in fact taking these actions. Two good general rules for children to follow are (1) limit personal information – addresses, phone numbers, and even schools' names or locations can put children at risk of unwanted face-to-face encounters; (2) use social networks that allow the child to designate who can log in and leave messages; these notes are referred to as "privacy notes." Adults should be reading and examining the "friends" in the network and discussing issues about a network friend with children, just as face-to-face friendships are. Be open, direct, and caring with the monitoring, just as with all interactions with the children.

This chapter's length does not allow for a summary of the homophobia, racism, and sexism depicted in the media, although there is a great deal of this content as well. We know that children's beliefs about these topics are related to media. Adolescents report that they use media as one of their top three or four resources for information of any kind. Adult filters of media are a resource for children as well. Talking with children about topics that interest them when they are ready is a "best line of defense" against inappropriate programming to children and is needed along with filtering. Adults can also show children how media can be a positive force, one that can be used to promote good Ph. Some positive media already exist.

Educational media began with *Sesame Street* almost forty years ago on public television. We know a bit about this positive influence. Educational, positive programming for children has greater effect sizes in research than violent programming (Hearold 1986). This statistical jargon simply means that researchers have found they can promote more prosocial behavior in children with positive programming than when they study children's interpersonal aggression after showing them violent programming. Wow! Let's do this! Unfortunately, just as I said when I began this section about media, the majority of media is not made for promoting children's cognitive and social development. Responsible adults can be activists for children's programming – for all programming for that matter – and filters for children in their care. It is a large responsibility, but one that is sorely needed.

In this chapter we have reviewed many sources that influence and educate children as they grow outside of the home. Good Ph begins at home, but external influences are also powerful in children's lives. Collaborative adults can make a difference in the cognitive growth of children. The cognitive and social stimulation that caregivers and teachers provide to children helps their continued positive development along pathways of psychological health. Adults in children's lives have much responsibility to help shape their environments for their optimal growth in childcare and other educational settings. This environmental framework that helps promote children's growth includes adults who act as filters for influences like media.

Childcare Notes

1 Cost of childcare varies a great deal due to types of care, quality, and even regions of the country. Non-maternal in-home care costs can range from small fees paid to relatives to licensed individuals operating businesses from their homes. As such, qualified care of infants by individuals often costs about $200–300 per week. Childcare centers for toddlers also vary. Quality centers can cost as much as $400 a week. Some centers that wish to promote a kind of "designer" appeal can cost as much as $650 a week. Other centers who are a part of a religious institution's mission or community activism can be very high in quality but much less in cost. Urban centers with high poverty rates can have state or subsidized childcare, some of high quality for low-income families (e.g., Project Head Start).

2 Some childcare centers accept infants as young as six weeks. Private individuals may accept younger infants. Carefully evaluate how this decision comprises a part of the "best parenting possible" concept.

3   Without wishing to make new parents anxious, it is still the case that many quality childcare centers and private individuals across the United States have waiting lists. After reviewing childcare options, consider a waiting list when pregnancies are in the second or third trimester. In this way, if the wait is six months to one year, there may be an opening that fits the time when families need it. Best practice, find out the waiting period for a quality environment and act accordingly as early as possible. Be advised that some childcare providers require a waiting list fee or deposit as well.

4   The Internet is one useful resource concerning childcare options. Remember, however, that adults without childcare skill can place themselves on the Internet as childcare experts. Find out the credentials of the web writer or web space owner. Other parents can be a resource for expectant parents. While mothers' and fathers' opinions are valuable, they usually are a reflection of their own experience. Try to get other useful data as well. For example, each state's website has many pages about childcare licensing and childcare in general.

5   General parenting information can be found on many websites. This could be regional like the "Berkeley Parents Network" in California or national like that provided by the Pew Charitable Trust and the National Institute for Early Education Research.

School Choice Notes

When adults examine possible school choices, whether public or private, large or small, questions such as the following can help in their evaluations.

1   In what way do school administrators and individual teachers communicate with parents? Are phone numbers and email addresses easily accessible? Are newsletters sent home or mailed?

2   Are parents viewed as collaborative partners with a presence on, for example, planning committees?

3   Are there opportunities for employed parents to meet with school staff?

4   How visible are community commitments to and collaborations with the schools (e.g., tax bases and other funding sources)?

Chapter 4

A Part of the Family: How Belonging Promotes Growth

◆ ◆ ◆

Quick! Name a television show about families that ran for ten years. Not *The Waltons*, not *The Cosby Show*. If you guessed *7th Heaven*, the longest running family drama in television history, you were correct. The actor who played the Reverend Camden and dad to seven children, Stephen Collins, says their success was due to a simple idea of the creators: celebrate families. Each episode was a fairly realistic look at parent, child, and sibling relationships. The viewer saw a snapshot of the strengths and foibles of each character and how these relationships affected the growth of each family member. Complexity was evident, solutions were not always easy or found, and yet family belongingness was central to the dialogue. Every family member knew that each was there for the other.

Recall that in chapters 2 and 3 we examined cognitive growth within the home and in external environments as the first two measures that predict children's good Ph. The third measure for positive Ph outcomes concerns the solid foundation a family can provide to children from all backgrounds. The social development of children begins in the home. Research about effective parenting and the reciprocity of parent-child relationships in the context of the family and other social systems is central to this chapter. Giving and receiving in family relationships are precursors of personal responsibility and positive relationships later in life. Children who contribute to a family's functioning by means of completing household tasks or who assist with planning a leisure activity feel included. Simple tools such as communicating effectively with children, making expectations and responsibilities clear, and using warmth to convey expectations all contribute to a child's sense of belonging to a family. Children who feel they belong to a functional family have a sense of self that will help them do well in other important environments, such as school. A solid family foundation that includes warmth and boundaries can be achieved. This is the concept I term *belonging*.

Psychologists know that by the time children reach adolescence or the teen years, they have a sense of family that can inoculate them against some poor decision-making concerning, for example, smoking, substance abuse, and sexual activity. These risky behaviors are a part of what adolescents must cope with, sometimes on a daily basis. Consider family relatedness as a good booster shot or inoculation to prevent behavior that puts children at risk for poor outcomes. Good Ph is the goal. If children feel a personal connection with their families or belonging, their sense of responsibility to themselves as well as to their families is evidenced in their behavior and their psychological health is strengthened.

Psychologists also know that this connection needs some purposive direction on the part of adults early in children's lives. The promotion of this relational skill-building is possible, very much within everyone's reach. However, family relationships are complex and do not exist in a vacuum. Other people and events outside of the family also exert some influence on children's development of relationships.

The Family as a System in Context

A family can be thought of as a complex relational system. The characteristics and development of one child are thought to be associated with the rest of the family members' characteristics and development. Moreover, this developing family system exists in a time frame with concomitant historical patterns that are associated with the culture. Institutions present in a society are imbued with power to transmit cultural prescriptions to families about values and behaviors thought to be the norm in the society.

Uri Bronfenbrenner, a pioneer in child development, considered the complexities of child development in relation to all other people and events in the children's lives. He called this framework the "ecological theory of development," meaning that various levels of influence or "systems" are embedded in each other and are reciprocal in nature: each affects the other (see Bronfenbrenner 1986). Figure 1 provides

Bronfenbrenner's Ecological Theory of Development

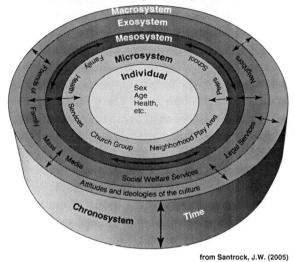

from Santrock, J.W. (2005)

Figure 1 Bronfenbrenner's ecological theory of development (from Santrock 2005).

an example of the family system from one child's perspective, as it is related to other systems where social skill-building is affected.

A child comes into a family by birth or adoption and interacts with other family members. The child eventually attends a school that will mean new people with whom he will interact, including teachers and peers. This school has rules about who can attend, who are educational partners, what is taught, etc., that are prescribed by cultural norms. For example, in the United States a cultural norm exists, a valued belief if you will, that every child deserves a public education and that parents are partners in children's education. This cultural prescription about the education of children is given to the institution of schools to carry out. The cultural prescription and hope is that teachers and parents interact to promote the education of the child. At the same time, historical events such as economic downturns in a society may mean less funding for schools, or unemployed parents. Both of these possible outcomes of economic losses will impact the education of children as well. Schools may cut funding or rearrange their funding priorities; unemployed parents may lack a means of transportation to the school or perhaps exhibit decreased parental functioning as a result of unemployment. These socio-historical patterns are related to child outcomes.

The concept of reciprocal processes also means that the very children we are examining and hoping to influence positively constitute one-half of our dyadic interactions with them. As children move from early childhood into the adolescent years, their needs change and parenting must change also. Parental control shifts as children develop more autonomy. For parents, this balancing of control and autonomy can be a formidable task.

Retaining the example above of the impact of parental unemployment, when a child becomes an adolescent, parental interest in school may seem like an incursion to him. An unemployed parent's anxiety about a child's performance at school may propel the parent to check with teachers often about his work. The child may argue against this parent's interactions with teachers. However, when children are minors or remain under the purview of parents as young people, adults retain the responsibility to decide how much influence should be exerted in external domains like that of school as children develop. Thus, a parent's decision concerning what amount of control to retain while granting some autonomy to the adolescent should be examined with an ecological perspective; that is, to what extent should the parent intervene in the school environment of the adolescent?

The ecological system level that includes parents interacting with teachers at the school can mean a positive outcome for children. For parents of adolescents, the child's autonomy needs should be considered. Parents can retain a positive relationship with adolescents and decide with discretion the extent to which talking with teachers about school factors is in the best interest of the child's development, even when adult issues such as unemployment loom large. The family system has reciprocal interactions with entities such as the context of school and economic stability. Communication between parents and teachers is advised for almost every eventuality. Family members and school personnel interact to assist the developing child.

Children who have a family to rely upon when they are young have that same family bond when they are adolescents. The questions or problems to solve often differ as the children grow, but the concept of belonging remains the same. Belonging can be considered the cornerstone of good Ph because of the nature of cognitive and social growth within the family environment.

The Development of Belonging and Induction

Adults can teach and promote this healthy state of belonging beginning in the children's early years, and continue throughout their development. Social skills such as reasoning about decision-making and compromise can be taught to children so that they are aware of their personal responsibility for their own behavior and family expectations about how their behavior affects others. Such knowledge helps children think independently when adults are not present. These effective strategies also provide a model for children of patience and caring. Reasoning with children about family expectations and explaining consequences of behavior and discipline decisions will help them govern their own behavior later. This reasoning strategy is called *induction*.

Induction simply means that adults who care about children use reasoning with discipline. This reasoning includes teaching children the concept of the consequences of their actions, hopeful that children will begin to understand and use this reasoning by themselves when adults are not present.

The Developing Parent

Where to begin? Adults in a family need information about their own views of parenting. Parents can begin by making an assessment of their skills and beliefs about childrearing and where these ideas originated. Of course, if *prospective* parents engage in these conversations or self-assessment, it is all the better. Child psychologist Diana Baumrind published results of years of her research in the early 1970s that showed how the use of both reasoning about expectations of behavior and warmth provide a solid foundation for children to become age-appropriately independent and eventually well-functioning adults (Baumrind 1971). Overall, there are two dimensions of parenting to consider: accepting vs. rejecting behaviors and demanding vs. lenient behaviors. The first dimension refers to the warmth the parent provides in the parent-child dyad and the second refers to the level and flexibility of demands that parents place on their children. These demands can also be thought of as expectations or standards of conduct.

Accepting children as valuable people who deserve respect and love, while at the same time demanding a standard of conduct with some flexibility, is the parenting method that researchers such as Baumrind recommend. The expectations of a standard of behavior, communicated with warmth, along with explanations about how these fit the values of a family set the child on a course for good Ph. Positive statements about the children's ability to reach a standard with the help of the caring adults in their lives provide messages about belonging and competence that will benefit children in all contexts of their development. Thus, we see that the neat combination of personal responsibility and relationships can be taught early and are so important to functioning families.

Finding the right combination of acceptance of the child and the appropriate level of expectation concerning children's behavior is not always easy for adults, however. For example, safety rules must be adhered to in many ways to help young children grow. They often require a high standard without leniency for young children. However, even strong rules about safety given with reasoning and warmth are possible.

Safety Example

Children cannot be allowed to play in the streets of many families' neighborhoods, especially in suburban areas where personal vehicles are the primary means of transportation. "Don't play in the street" is a demand that parents with very young children often make. This safety demand can be given with warmth and reasoning, accepting the child as a valuable human being on his own, separate from his behaviors. However, if young children do not obey this rule, strong verbal and behavioral messages on the part of parents are warranted. In this instance, the parents' demand for the children's safety behavior takes priority over allowing them to figure out safe behaviors on their own. Children playing in the street can mean physical injury. Their size inhibits drivers' views of them and the children are poor thinkers about others' behaviors; young children often may not know how to get out of a dangerous situation. This is one example where lenience is not advised. Yet strong verbal messages about staying in the yard to play can be given with caring, even if a "time-out" is warranted inside.

Corporal Punishment

Some parents may feel that spanking a disobedient child who is engaging in unsafe behaviors is appropriate. A discussion about corporal punishment is needed here. Across studies in psychology, researchers use different definitions of corporal punishment. It is generally agreed, however, that corporal punishment includes a range of behaviors, from hitting a child's buttocks with an open palm to physical abuse that causes injury. How to define corporal punishment with demarcations about injury, whether emotional or physical, is difficult and is related to socio-historical forces. Bronfenbrenner's (1986) ecological systems theory again serves as a useful framework to examine these forces or levels of influence in the family. The historical and social contexts of corporal punishment in the United States, as well as the decisions adults make about whether to use corporal punishment, are related to children's outcomes and their Ph.

Historical Patterns

Historically, many Americans practice corporal punishment as part of an Anglo-European tradition that has been supported through religious teachings. English Common Law in Britain allowed men to use corporal punishment to control their wives and children, as though they were chattel or men's property. These laws helped form the basis of the legal system in the United States. In the North American colonies in the 1700s, corporal punishment was prevalent in parents' attempts to control and teach their children. Corporal punishment meant any kind of physical discipline, including a range of behaviors from hitting and public whipping to injuring children permanently.

Corporal punishment within families remained prevalent in the nineteenth century and through much of the twentieth. However, with the advent of two large social movements in the United States – the Civil Rights Movement in the 1960s and the Feminist Movement in the 1970s – more attention was paid to the family and oppression of any kind. Children's rights were examined in ways heretofore neglected. Corporal punishment came under close scrutiny by the state, and legislation was enacted to protect children from their caregivers who might abuse them, whether parents or unrelated individuals such as teachers. Corporal punishment became associated with child abuse.

The incidence of corporal punishment in the United States in the 1970s was quite high. In an often-referenced study published by Straus, Gelles, and Steinmetz in 1980, 71 percent of the parents surveyed reported that they hit their children, while 20 percent said they did so with objects. One-fourth of the mothers in the study reported that they hit their children before they were six months of age, and this figure rose to nearly one-half by the time the children had reached the age of 12 months.

Corporal Punishment and Adult Responsibility

Corporal punishment of children is still allowed in the United States, but the line between teaching and abuse is often difficult to discern. Parents who believe that corporal punishment is an effective disciplinary technique may begin to hit a child in the name of good parenting, but get out of control and hurt the child physically or psychologically as they model a technique of control promoted by fear.

Parents who use corporal punishment may be approached by law enforcement personnel or other state officials to answer questions about their parenting. They may have charges brought against them by the state. If cases of child abuse are substantiated, a range of outcomes is possible. Caseworkers employed by the state may decide to work with affected families to increase parents' skill level, or children may be removed from the home if future injury appears to be likely.

Legally, every adult citizen of the United States is required to report suspected cases of child abuse. Realize that the "suspected cases" phrase means that lay people are not expected to be able to ascertain or verify suspected cases. Rather, a report to the Child Abuse Hotline means that a professional who *has* been trained to examine suspected cases will be sent to the home. Anonymity on the part of the reporter is hoped for and upheld by the state, but may not always be supported. For example, a neighbor may question others about who made a report of suspected abuse. However, at the level of personal ethics, standing up for a child is important to whole societies. In the United States, report suspected cases of child abuse to the Child Abuse Hotline at 1–800–422–4453.

In the late 20th century, corporal punishment in the home accounted for 60 percent of the corroborated incidences of child abuse in the United States. In a Gallop poll survey conducted in 1994, 46 percent of adults agreed that sometimes children need a "good, hard spanking" (Hall 1998). However, by 2004, that belief in the power of corporal punishment was decreasing in the United States. For example, pediatrician Michael Regalado and his colleagues found that only 26 percent of their sample reported spanking their three- and four-year-old children, but these did so frequently (Regalado et al. 2004). By a comparison of these data from the last thirty years, it appears that a belief in the effectiveness of corporal punishment is waning in the United States. A cultural prescription of discipline with reasoning and warmth appears to be on the rise. However, because standardized methods of research are rarely used across studies, this apparent trend may be an artifact of different research designs. Should these data portend a trend, these changing social attitudes toward corporal punishment mean that parents, who may once have thought that their disciplinary rights included the right to hit, slap, or punch their children, will have to shift to other forms of discipline for teaching and punishing their children.

Because corporal punishment has a long legacy of social support in the United States, it may be difficult for parents to employ other methods of teaching. A generation of parents who used corporal punishment may try to undermine the efforts of new parents who wish to employ other discipline techniques. However, parents who know no discipline techniques except corporal punishment can learn new skills.

Precursors to Corporal Punishment

How does the use of corporal punishment develop? Strife in existing relationships in families when children are born may not bode well for the children. Conflict between family members may mean corporal punishment of their offspring is more likely. For example, a study published in the *Journal of Family Psychology* by Korrell Kanoy and her colleagues found that marital conflict and couples' hostility prior to the birth of a child is related to the couples' use of corporal punishment after their children are born. High hostility between married pairs is related to the high use of corporal punishment of their children (Kanoy et al. 2003).

While the social values of modern culture may reject injury to children and assert that most corporal punishment is unnecessary, many adults still uphold their rights as parents to use corporal punishment and do not view their behavior to be abusive in any way. For example, some religious sects approve and encourage corporal punishment of children by adults in the home and use their interpretations of religious texts to support their behavior. Some adults who can be grouped along a dimension in the United States such as class or ethnic origin are thought to use corporal punishment more than others. For example, Vonnie McLoyd, an expert in children at risk for poor outcomes, found that some families who must rear their children in poverty environments may resort to corporal punishment surrounding safety issues because of the inherent dangerousness of their neighborhood. Corporal punishment may be an adaptation to extreme environments (see Harrison-Hale et al. 2004).

Other social factors outside of the home also contribute to our understanding of corporal punishment. Violent acts in the media, fictionalized and real, are ingested daily by adults and children. These messages, combined with corporal punishment in the home, provide one model of social interaction to children that may effect their development.

A country's laws can prohibit or promote corporal punishment. Looking cross-culturally we find groups whose views about the use of corporal punishment differ from the laws of the United States. For example, Scandinavian countries have treated the corporal punishment of children as illegal for many decades. Their reasoning is that since physical aggression toward one's neighbor is illegal, adults' conduct toward their children should be held to the same level of accountability. While diverse voices may be heard on the subject of corporal punishment, there exists research suggesting that corporal punishment is negatively related to children's positive outcomes or good Ph.

Outcomes of Corporal Punishment

Developmental data suggest that children are adversely affected by corporal punishment. Children mimic their caregivers. They see adults modeling a behavior and they are very likely to repeat it. Researchers such as Albert Bandura (1965) have shown that such modeling of aggressive behaviors serves to show children several logical links with outcomes. Modeling physical aggression conveys to children the messages that when they are angry, they may hit others; that when they are bigger, they may hit others and get away with it; and that physical aggression is a form of behavior to be repeated for a desirable outcome, getting one's way, having power over another, etc. Physical aggression becomes one way to communicate with others.

Those children whose parents practice corporal punishment are the most physically aggressive toward their peers, according to several researchers (e.g., Kazdin and Benjet 2003). Modeling is one of the most powerful teaching tools adults have and modeling corporal punishment is related to aggression in children. Children from such homes can develop negative interactions at school and fewer cooperative techniques for their interactions in other social settings. Subsequent rejection by peers and teachers may put children at risk for developing larger problems. Thus, children who have been slapped and hit by their parents will be vulnerable to failure in the school setting. School failure has been linked to antisocial disorders, including delinquency, school drop out and later, adult criminality. For these reasons, most psychologists agree that it is important for new parents and those couples who are considering parenthood to examine their own childhood histories and discuss forms of discipline that do not employ corporal punishment. However, it is important to note one caveat about these data: the nature of correlational research. A correlation of two factors simply means that they are related in some way.

Psychologists Alan Kazdin and Corina Benjet caution that the causal effects of corporal punishment are unknown; only relationships between factors such as corporal punishment and peer-to-peer aggression have been shown. While we may posit that corporal punishment in the home begins before peer aggression at school, it is also possible that peer aggression at school means the child will receive corporal punishment at home for that behavior. The two factors vary together: when one behavior increases, the other rises also. However, when these data are taken together, the next question should be about how to support parents so that corporal punishment is not employed.

Alternative Discipline Techniques

The goals of many parents include how to keep their families healthy and happy. A sense of belonging promotes social relationships both inside and outside of the family. For parents who wish to promote that sense of belonging, discipline techniques exist that do not include hitting a child. These non-corporal techniques have wide support in psychology as to their effectiveness. Praise for good behavior is an alternative proactively administered before punishment is even warranted. Reasoning with a child about how the good behavior impacts him and others positively makes explicit the links between personal behavior and relationships. Reasoning about bad behaviors after some noncompliance is another alternative to corporal punishment.

Removing a child from a reinforcing environment is another strategy that can be used and discussed with a child. For example, time-out from playing aggressively with peers may give the child time to reflect and calm down. (See chapter 2 about tips for the use of time-out.) Fines on a behavior chart or a lessoning of freedoms can be used. For example, "grounding" the child to the home for a period of time concomitant with the noncompliance may also give him time to reflect about his behavior. He will likely desire a return to contact with peers such that he monitors and controls his own aggression when future opportunities arise. Taken together, these strategies for handling children's behavior are excellent and effective, without worry about physical or emotional injury to the child.

There are organizations that can help adults be effective parents without the use of corporal punishment. Organizations such as the American Humane Association Children's Division is one such source that helps provide parenting support and education to people who do not wish to use corporal punishment. The online resource called "Project No Spank" can be found at www.nospank.net/toc/htm. Counseling centers at universities can provide parenting support or refer parents to other resources. Local mental health care providers are also an excellent information resource. Finding one family resource usually means that these professionals have access to other local counseling and education groups who support parents. A supported parent can be an effective parent, one who promotes personal responsibility, relationships, and belonging. Those parents who know only corporal punishment as their discipline technique can learn new skills. Skilled parenting without corporal punishment is possible, especially when parents feel supported by important others in their lives and by their society in general.

Effective Parenting

We return to the picture of the skilled parent who promotes feelings of belongingness. Remember that this parent accepts the child as a loved, respected individual, yet expects adherence to rules, appropriate for the child's age. According to Baumrind (1971) and researchers like her, parents who apply both warmth and a standard of behavior also engage in other healthy parental behaviors. Parents who promote feelings of belongingness do so by means of the following strategies with their children. These guidelines are supported with data from psychology.

Guidelines for promoting belonging
1 Parental control and child autonomy are balanced. Opportunities for decisions about behavior are given to children, but this granting of independence is age appropriate and is monitored.
2 Standards of behavior are clear and guidance for reaching them is given.
3 Discussion about decisions, even disciplinary decisions, is allowed. This discussion serves as a model for other social relationships.
4 Consequences of misbehavior are congruent with the behavior. Explaining the relationship of act and consequence is another reasoning tool children will use later.

5 Parental warmth in the teaching of boundaries promotes recep-
   tiveness to learning in the child. Mutual obligations are made
   explicit.
6 Asking the child to problem-solve through a previously poor
   decision promotes this reasoning skill (e.g., "What might you try
   the next time you and your friend disagree?"). Offer suggestions
   relevant to the age of the child.
7 Praise and support of children's appropriate behavior is explicit.
8 Parental conflict with others is noted and not brought to bear on
   the child (e.g., marital conflict).
9 Parent-as-role-model means that adults are cognizant of their
   own behavior and act with integrity. They show congruence
   between spoken standards and their own behavior.
10 Parental teaching is proactive. Potential problems are averted
   and discussed.

While the above list is not exhaustive concerning an effective parent,
these guidelines are a resource for the many examples of daily living
problems and events that are inherent in families. Parents' willingness
to practice these strategies will help children become functioning
adults. With such a solid foundation with which to begin, children
will pass on feelings of belongingness when they become parents. For
adults who wish to practice these guidelines, remember that modeling
positive behaviors in relationships is a wonderful tool.

Readers who were previously unaware of these guidelines may still
have had a good beginning with their children which these guidelines
can strengthen. Practical applications of the guidelines by means of
the following examples should prove helpful.

Practice in Daily Living

Families have day-to-day responsibilities that they must complete. While
children need free time that includes play and creativity opportunities,
they also need practice with being a contributing part of the family. This
is not a blank check to burden children with many adult responsibilities, but their efforts can make a difference to the smooth functioning
of a family. However, some families, because of economic necessity,
may require many tasks of their children. Not all families have the

luxury of teaching children family responsibilities slowly, but expectations made with warmth make relationship-building central to the work of all families. With warmth and guidance, children with many tasks can thrive as well.

If it is possible for a family to use moderation with task assignments, tasks should begin as simple ones and become more complex as the children develop. These tasks are also called "chores" or "housework." Explaining to children why schedules are important and how they can help in the home is one place to begin. Giving them some choices with these household tasks is more practice that increases their competence and confidence-building. Begin these lessons when a child is mobile. Work with the child; model the desired behavior. Toddlers can easily be taught to put away toys, take their cups to the kitchen, that sort of housework. Children may resist, but calmly explain that it takes everyone in a family to keep a family running smoothly. Say to the child, "You are a part of this family, we need everyone to pitch in. I'll help you today." By teaching a child that there are many tasks to do in a day that do not take much time but that make everyone's day go a little better, adults are giving the child a chance to contribute to the family in a concrete way.

By the time children are around four or five years of age they can understand weekly assignments, even more so when adults are engaged in the same behavior. This age child can put things away, dust, etc. These tasks are up to parents to decide, but remember that if the children have choices presented to them, their sense of control and belonging is supported as well. Because of the child's age, the task may not be done perfectly. Helping children learn skills to complete household chores may take more time for the parents than simply completing all tasks by themselves. However, the teaching of these tasks is related to the parent and child relationship-building as well.

Noting the children's strengths and weaknesses will help adults know what kinds of tasks to assign or offer as alternatives. For example, a child who has difficulty with small hand and finger movements ("fine motor skill") may benefit from folding simple angles, like those on washcloths. Encouragement and patience are key to helping children master these new skills. Allow choices and room for improvement. Thank the children for their help. Everyone enjoys praise for a job well done and children are no exception.

Psychologists know that asking children to complete age-appropriate tasks in the home promotes a sense of family. Play and work in the home are integral to a family's functioning. As the children develop, their involvement in questions families grapple with becomes another teaching tool available to adults.

Practice in Problem-Solving

Family problem-solving, compromise, and commitment are all a part of being in a family. Family members need each other to get the business of the family done, as well as to share fun activities. Family problem-solving does not necessarily mean that a negative problem exists, it simply means that together, a family will work toward an agreed upon goal. As usual, begin as early as possible. Children should be included in family problem-solving about work activities as well as leisure activities at an early age. While one child's needs should be a focus of a family, keep in mind that parents and other children in a family have needs too, as well as extended family members or friendship group members. Each family system can be large and complex.

Problem-solving is a necessary part of many decisions a family makes. While a middle school-aged child has some skill at how to consider options that look the best for him, the teaching of family relatedness with those options is needed throughout childhood and adolescent development as well. Dependent on how many children, parents, and grandparents live together, many family members may be involved in decision-making. This is the essence of being a part of a family, listening to everyone's needs, and trying to find solutions that best fit the whole family. Compromise is made explicit. Each person's needs are supported from time to time or parts of each person's needs are met usually. By providing everyone in a family a voice, belongingness is supported.

Practice at Play!

First, when adults talk to infants daily the children come to know that important others care about their welfare. A response to their needs in an even temper with explanations makes explicit a message that adults share their desire for comfort and wish to assist them as they grow. Caring for infants with warmth and concern models a first relationship to them. When children are around one year of age, adults can begin to offer choices to them. These choices should be simple, but made available. For the child who is 18 months of age, offering to read one book or another is a neat tactic to show the child he has a voice about his welfare. Psychologists state that this kind of choice availability teaches a child agency, or power, in his environment. His needs are important and his wishes are solicited and supported within reason. For the child who is two to three years of age, the choices adults provide can be a bit more complex. For example, adults can suggest two fun activities to a child, appropriate to the age of the child. Of course, when providing choices to children, adults must commit to carrying out either of the activities presented to the child. These choices are a great way for children to feel included, and give the child an early view of what being a part of a family is all about.

Messy Play Time Example

If a parent thinks that a messy play time sounds fun, she or he can ask the child which sounds better, finger-painting or mud pies. Again, both of these choices must be possible with the adult's commitment. Once the child makes a decision about which messy play activity sounds fun, begin it as soon as possible. Be prepared ahead of time to start the preparation for the fun activity with the child as soon as the child decides. Enjoy the activity with the child. Interactions during play are often times for parents to learn about joys and fears that have not been spoken by young children before. Praise the child's efforts, be directive in some ways but not in others. For example, perhaps keeping the messiness on a table is necessary, but building and breaking down are allowed. Depending on the age of the child, he may tire of the fun quickly and ask for another activity. Teaching a child focus is a good lesson as well; try to keep the child engaged with other aspects of the activity. For example, finger-painting one picture usually leads to three or four. They may all look the same or each look different. If the young child is engaged, he is likely finding delight in the activity.

However, for the early childhood age group, a fun activity that lasts 20 minutes or beyond should be considered a success. If the child is adamant about shifting to another activity and their time together is limited, this is a good time for adults to teach outcomes of choices (consequences of behavior) and moderation. The activity may have to end, but adults can structure days so that a messy play time is sure to come around again. At that next opportunity, adults should again ask with some guidance, "Do you want to play with mud pies this time? Last time we finger-painted and you said you'd like to try the mud pies." Depending on the maturity of the child, you may be playing with finger-paints again; repetition is a part of the young child's practice with the world. The lesson is simply that the child has some control, chooses an activity, has some structure with an adult, and enjoys the outcome.

If more than one child has been a part of the decision-making and fun activity, perhaps compromise was arrived at early to begin the activity. If one child's wishes were supported on the first messy play day, the other child's first choice can be the next fun activity. Children see that compromise works and that their needs are important. Make these links explicit for the children. State the agreement, remind the children of it, carry through with it. Tell the children that compromise is a part of relationships and that each person's wishes are important. Adults' commitment to these relationship agreements models a behavior that children need to establish as part of their own.

Developing Social Skills for Maturation

Family belonging means that everyone's needs are important. Personal responsibility and relationships are supported that promote good Ph. When adults attend to children's needs with a balance of structure and freedom, the children are learning that adults care about them, that problem-solving and choices can be fun, and that they have some control over their environments. This kind of decision-making without much risk means that lessons about future decisions, independent of adults, will build upon the first. By the time the children are adolescents, talking about choices, thinking about alternatives and outcomes, will be a part of their behaviors. Look at this example of a young child who was allowed to decide upon a summer camp.

Child Chooses Mud!

A mom allowed her five year old to choose a morning summer camp activity for one week. The two discussed the local library's program and the beach program choices. The mom discussed with her child that he had gone to the library's camp in the previous summer and learning about beach critters would be a new activity. He happily chose the beach summer camp and his week went well. Beach camp excursions included shell collecting and handling fish, big and small. On the last day of camp the mom picked up her very mud-covered child and asked how he was doing. The grumpy boy replied, "I wish I'd gone to the library!" Apparently, the marsh was that morning's discovery environment and the camp staff did not supervise the children to clean off the caked-on mud that had been there for a few hours. The mom suppressed a laugh and said warmly to her boy, "We'll get you cleaned up soon and you might feel better." Later in the day, the child said to his mom, "I loved beach camp!"

The boy in the example chose an activity and had one uncomfortable time frame that motivated him to reconsider his choice. This is understandable, for all of us can experience similar events. However, for a five year old, a simple cleaning up for his own physical comfort helped him make another assessment of his choice later in the day. The mom could have taken time to discuss the nature of choices that often includes some positive and negative components, but for this five year old, allowing the child to do his own reassessment was also valuable.

Allowing children to make choices also means helping them learn about poor choices or those that do not work out so well. This important lesson is simply allowing consequences for children's choices and behavior. If the child chooses an activity that does not have such a good ending, let the child know that there will be other chances and that making choices is no guarantee of brilliance each time one is made. Remind the child that as humans we cannot know outcomes of each choice prior to an activity much of the time. We learn about the world by trying new things. Adults should not overburden children with repetitions about what they may see as a "bad choice." Rather, when adults refrain from this negative behavior it is a message that learning about the world includes a bit of risk.

Problem-solve about how to best tackle the next fun play time or activity. Discuss how to examine alternatives. Allowing children to experience the outcomes of decisions they have made will teach many valuable lessons. This practice teaches children the consequences of their choices. It teaches that choosing from an array can be difficult but rewarding and the child is viewed as a competent, growing person with skills to learn. This kind of permission is a very strong statement of their being a part of the family. Others' acceptance of our mistakes and foibles, along with our triumphs, is likely the best part about belonging.

As discussed in the messy play time example, compromise among family members is another strategy that healthy families employ to promote belongingness. Again, from a very early age, children can be taught this valuable tool to help them make and sustain positive relationships. Considering the examples given above, a young child may demand that both mud pies and finger-painting activities must occur on a given day. Adults' considerations of others who need them in the family may require the parents to parcel their time between several family members. The parent can say, "Let's compromise and do one activity now. I promise we will have another chance to play like this very soon." Stating such a long word as "compromise" to a toddler may seem odd, but early use of important words like this helps children learn what is important to the adults in a family. As children develop, compromise becomes a part of their interactions with others and they come to expect that relationships include give and take that benefits all parties. This reciprocity of relationships promotes a sense of belonging in families and children's social development is facilitated.

When children reach their adolescent years, compromise and family negotiations may take on a whole new complexity for everyone in a family. However, these building blocks of belonging are present and children know their family's commitment to them.

Practice in Adolescence

During the adolescent years, the commitment to family belongingness may require more flexibility as more autonomy is expected by the adolescent. Along with the adolescent's expectations, parents expect responsible decision-making to increase and higher commitment to the self and others as priorities for the adolescents. Problem-solving about alternatives to come to a decision may require much input from the adolescent in order for him to feel valued and competent. One effective tool with adolescents is the concept of "brainstorming" alternative actions to reach an important decision. Brainstorming can be used with children who are in elementary school, also, but the adolescent can use it with more skill. Adolescents are much more competent than younger children at considering several alternatives at one time and the expected outcomes of each. This is a part of the adolescent's more advanced thinking skills.

Adolescents may experience difficulties with others in the home; perhaps their siblings are disrespectful of boundaries concerning ownership and the use of valued items such as electronics. Outside of the home adolescents may experience difficulty with others concerning friendship issues or with school decisions concerning, for example, how to choose between athletics and music in a school curriculum. Parents often need to guide decisions about topics of this importance, but practice at brainstorming may be helpful to all who participate, including the adults. The rules for brainstorming with children are the following:

1 Make the family an integral part of the process. Both the issues and the children's maturity levels must be assessed and monitored as adults decide who can participate.
2 Seek commitment to the process by all involved before beginning.
3 State the rules for brainstorming together. They are: the problem is agreed upon, each person suggests an alternative to deal with the problem, no interruptions, no negatives. Adults may wish to keep a written list, especially if young children need scaffolding.
4 One adult states: "You now have a list of possible actions to take. Let's discuss the pros and cons of each." Discussion should follow

in a somewhat systematic way, depending on the ages of all participating.

5   One adult states: "With these possibilities, which one will you try?" If the child is unsure, the adult can state: "Think about these and make a decision by [a negotiated date]. At that time we can discuss which one you chose and how you'll carry it out."

6   Let the child know that an agreement to act carries with it a commitment to do so.

7   Parents can say if they believe the alternative action chosen by the child is a mistake. Say so clearly and with warmth.

8   Allow the child the chance to try the chosen alternative if safety or other important considerations have been dealt with or are not a part of the problem.

9   Check with the child about the outcome and discuss. Avoid repetitions about a "bad decision." Rather, remind the child of the value of trying and learning.

10 If more than one family member is involved with a chosen alternative and the action is not carried out or is thwarted, meet again to discuss prior commitment.

Family Development

Valuable lessons learned through early decision-making and compromise in a family help us develop in many ways. When people experience cognitive, social, emotional, and behavioral practice that translates into mastering the environment and remaining connected to others, their psychological health is supported. Good Ph for children and adolescents often means good Ph for the adults in a family as well.

Increasing parental skill is possible for all adults. With effective parenting techniques and a focus on relationship development, families are built and supported. When children experience family belongingness they will be better able to make decisions when adults are not present. Perhaps the most threatening of these situations will not come until children reach the adolescent period. This period means much more freedom from adults, and practice thinking through options independently could literally be a life-saver for some adolescents. Situations such as sexual activity, underage drinking, and driving safety present opportunities for independent and competent children to use their problem-solving abilities that adults have taught them. Do not underestimate the importance of this ability. It is another positive basis for all development. As a functioning, thinking part of the family, the child will contribute to the overall health of the family, as well.

Play and work in the home are integral to a family's functioning. Beginning with infants and toddlers, belongingness means participating fully in a family. Teaching children how responsibilities and relationships work in tandem gives them a solid foundation for their later development. Parental expectations about standards of behavior, problem-solving, compromise, and commitment made with warmth and encouragement help children see possibilities for themselves and their relationships. Good Ph in children is related to their sense of belonging.

Families can differ by virtue of economic background, religion, or ethnicity, but a sense of belonging to a family is important for everyone. Adults must find a balance between control and autonomy as they parent their children. Psychologists believe that granting autonomy along with early teaching and models of behavior are good strategies for building competence in children that will transfer to domains outside of the family. Good Ph that begins at home is a correlate of children's healthy social development with their peers.

Chapter 5

Social Growth and Peer Relationships

◆ ◆ ◆

Colleen, a twelve year old, is riding in her mom's car and announces, "I'm so lucky to have so many good friends!" The mom asks her to tell her a little bit more about that, hoping to elicit more information and reflection upon the neat insight her daughter has just shared with her:

COLLEEN: "Well, I have more than ten friends at two different schools. Girls and boys like me."
MOM: "How do you think you got so lucky?"
COLLEEN: [somewhat exasperated] "I don't know!"
MOM: "I think your friendships are a marker of who you are."
COLLEEN: "What?"
MOM: "You are kind, trustworthy, fun, and smart. Other children like being with you for many reasons. You are a good friend to others."
COLLEEN: "Maybe."

By the end of this dialogue, Colleen is thoughtful but ready to move on to another topic. Perhaps her mom's gentle coaching about self-reflection was all Colleen wanted to hear at that moment. Perhaps she needed some time to consider her mom's views of her and whether they fit her own views of herself as a friend. Notice that Colleen's responses were still lacking in self-reflection beyond counting and categorizing her friends. This is not unusual for a twelve year old, yet "lucky Colleen" has absolutely contributed to her good fortune and good friendships.

In this chapter, I will focus on how peer relationships can promote the development of children and their good Ph. The fourth measure for psychologically healthy children concerns friendships and peer acceptance or rejection. Children's social growth and cognitive growth are beautifully intertwined, as we discussed in the previous chapters. The parent-child dyad is the first model for relationships that children encounter and these serve as patterns or frameworks for later relationships. Early socialization in the family is a good environment for learning about the self and others and helps children navigate the broader contexts of peer groups that follow. Adults in children's lives are very important to this growth, but peers constitute another pathway of relating to others and the world in general.

Social growth begins in infancy. Remember the first time the nursing infant in chapter 2 focused on his mother and seemed to note her presence in a way she had not seen before? The infant's focus was a manifestation of his cognitive and social growth at that moment. As infants develop they also begin to understand themselves as separate from others. This early cognizance of the "social other" simply means that an awareness of personal volition, separate from the behavior of others, is possible. For example, infants come to understand that they can act upon their environment, including drawing the caregiver into their proximity for care or play.

The early social relationships in a family give children information about interactions in general. These early relationships help people increase their ability to communicate and develop and maintain relationships. This skill is called relational or social competence. Relational competence sets children upon a positive path for future success in school and work environments, even into adulthood. Susan Harter, a psychologist who is expert on the role of the social other and personal self-esteem, says that the positive appraisals of others predict an individual's own positive self-esteem (see Harter 1999). Such self-esteem is related to good Ph.

Humans are social creatures whose surviving and thriving are very dependent upon their social competence. Children and adults use the information from others to help them see themselves, at least from a perspective separate from their own. This perspective or "social validation" transmits information to the individual about a variety of topics. How do others see me? How does their view compare with my own? How am I connected to others? What is my place in the world and how do I contribute? Social others assist with these complex, philosophical questions human beings wrestle with. Further, peers and friends give children a chance to interact on a more equal footing than their interactions with adults in their lives. Children understand that adults have more power in their relationships than they do. Peers provide that first step toward understanding the self in a reciprocal relationship with equal power.

In this chapter I will use "social others" to mean all people who are present in an individual's environment. "Peers" will denote a smaller group of children who share a commonality such as age or class mates, while "friends" will denote those individuals with whom personal, important information and time are shared. Friendship implies a mutuality or even conscious effort to become friends with reciprocity that leads to intimacy. For young children, friendship often means those children who play and enjoy similar activities either alongside or in concert with others and later in coordinated, complex dyads or triads. By early adolescence, children continue to seek friends for sharing enjoyable activities, but they also begin to seek close relationships for the purpose of learning about the self and others in a dyad of trust. Like twelve-year-old Colleen, many young adolescents cannot describe complex reasons for having friends, but they are beginning to question how friendships are formed and maintained and how they serve them as they grow. Children's overall development and good Ph relies a great deal on their social skill. I will use the terms "social competence" and "relational competence" interchangeably to mean positive skills exhibited when relating to others.

Parent-Child Framework

The first parent-child relationships serve as frameworks for all of the relationships people develop over their lifetimes. While we know that variability can occur because of many factors, psychologists agree that the model for behaving with others begins with parents. In chapter 4 we looked at the depth of importance that family belongingness has on young children's lives. Let us now examine how the parent-child relationship predicts peer relationships in general.

From a strict modeling perspective – that is, "children repeat what they see" – parents have a great deal of influence on the relationships of their children. Children will approach others with a model or framework of their relationships with their parents as their guide. For example, children who are used to parental warmth, boundaries, and expectations of behavior will approach peers with the same posi-tive expectations. These children are seen as socially competent by their peers and social others such as their teachers, and are usually successful with their attempts at interaction.

Social competence means that children have a set of skills that facil-itates their interactions with others; their relationships are built upon solid, direct communication that indicates concern for the self and for others. Often, this relational competence means that children also likely have good self-esteem, less chance of depressive symptoms or anxiety, and report greater life satisfaction than children without rela-tional competence (see Baumeister et al. 2003). Adolescents with good relational competence are less aggressive and dependent and more sympathetic toward others than their unskilled peers (see Dodge 1993). While most of the findings concerning relational competence are from studies about middle-income, Caucasian children in the United States, similar results have been found multiculturally in groups as diverse as Dutch and Turkish children (see Winstead 2004).

However, experts on the role of parents and their children's relational competence and overall development state that the lack of information about ethnic minority children in the United States means that we have only an incomplete picture concerning children's peer relationships. While low income and ethnic minority status are not synonymous, recall that a higher percentage of ethnic minority children live in poverty than Caucasian children in the United States. A few studies exist concerning ethnic minority children from low-income urban schools and their parent and peer relationships. Here are a few things we know based on this research. Parent involvement at school predicts peer success (see Cochran and Davila 1992). Authoritarian parents or those with strict rules have children with positive classroom behavior. Parents' and teachers' ratings of relational competence at school are often congruent, meaning the adults in the children's lives agree about their level of relational competence.

Research comparisons of relationship competence in European-American and ethnic minority children have shown "mixed results." This simply means that sometimes the children look quite similar and at other times they differ. For example, results have shown that among both European-American and ethnic minority children, higher involve-ment of parents with their children is related to greater peer success. However, they can differ in important ways in other studies. For example, African-American children have better peer relationships if their parents are stricter than European-American children's parents (Cochran and Davila 1992). We know very little about ethnic minority children's development of social competence, and adults interested in the concept of parent and peer relationship congruence should remember that generalizing to all children in the United States is ill-advised until we have a better database from which to draw.

Research concerning poverty and its relationship to children's social competence is fairly new, but some results apply to all children. Judy Dunn, a psychologist who is expert on children's friendships, states that low social status or poverty can have negative effects on children in predictable ways. Stress on families due to poverty can manifest in many ways that are related to children's friendships. For example, children who are reared in poverty may move often as one way to avoid homelessness. Lack of housing stability means less opportunity for children to develop friendships. An unstable neighborhood may put children at a safety risk and thus they are not allowed to play with their peers. Adult caregivers may have difficulty monitoring their children's peer relationships because of the adults' economic necessity of having two or more low-paying jobs. A lack of transportation for children to get together with friends is another practical consideration for families in poverty. Combine any of these factors with the negative events that may have led to poverty (e.g., employment lay-offs, family dysfunction, etc.) and the difficulties children from low-income families face in order to develop and maintain stable, positive peer relationships are obvious (Dunn 2004).

Despite inherent difficulties for some children, many children do enjoy the company of their peers. These early peer relationships are good practice for later relationships, including friendships and mating. Psychologists believe that the child who is socially competent is on a good Ph path.

Peers

Peer acceptance is not the same as friendship, for children can be popular with their classmates or peers, yet have only one or two classmates who qualify as friends. However, peer acceptance has great influence on children's development and deserves a discussion on its own. Positive peer interactions are the next building block for the social development of children after the parent-child relationship. These positive interactions will lead to friendships and later to strong ties that constitute mating and lifelong friendship commitments. Peer acceptance is another of those constructs that signal the merging of cognitive and social skill development in children. Developmental psychologists have examined peer interactions with both cognitive and social skill factors in mind as they study young children. The field is as complex as any human interaction. Further, adults in children's lives are responsible for promoting social growth by means of interventions as simple as getting a playgroup of children together, to monitoring and filtering adolescents' interactions with their peers.

Children's peer acceptance or rejection tells a story of overall development and predicts adult functioning as well. Social competence is not easily reduced to a set of behaviors, but we do know several skills that are seen in young children who develop positive peer relationships. While this list is not exhaustive in detail, it is a good snapshot of the developing social skills necessary for good Ph. Note too that cognitive skill accompanies each social skill listed.

Social skills for peer acceptance
1   Interest in others, a willingness to participate.
2   Self-regulation that is age appropriate (e.g., ability to focus, to wait).
3   Aggression control, both instrumental (e.g., taking another child's toy) and physical (e.g., hitting another child).
4   Perspective-taking: noting that others' views may differ from one's own.
5   Sense of fairness with behaviors such as sharing and turn-taking.
6   Emotional understanding: the ability to note various emotions and eventually link them with previous events or feeling states.
7   Positive self-perception (e.g., beliefs about personal social competence and the ability to use it to join others in activities).
8   Social responsivity that signals cooperation, noting and responding to feedback from others.
9   Behavioral flexibility that signals cooperation, a willingness to shift behaviors.
10 Social problem-solving: the ability to note conflict and use skills to help resolve it.

What an enormous amount of skill children must develop in order to have positive peer relationships! This mastery set has many complex parts to it. Developmentally, children usually increase their skill level as they age. Older children or those with more maturity than others in a group often exhibit greater social skill with peers than younger children. To make matters even more complex, peer relationships are dynamic and evolving. They often concern groups of children who differ from one context to another. For example, a preschool child who tends toward shyness may play at home with neighborhood children who are her peers with ease. However, when she enters the new setting of the school, the shy child may take weeks to join playgroups that include her neighborhood peers.

Social skills with peers are also predicated on other attributes like physical ability and communication competence. Children with disabilities may have various levels of deficit in one area or another that predict social competence difficulties. I will discuss a few of these possibilities as we examine the social skill list more closely.

Interest

Children who are comfortable in their environments, those who explore objects and people with visible enjoyment, are the children who will approach peers with interest. Even children as young as six to nine months old will respond differently to children than to adults. How do they know more fun will follow? We do not know! However, it is a neat marker of their interest in other children and the beginnings of peer relationships. Not all children possess this interest, due to a variety of factors such as neurological deficits or a lack of parental bonds. For example, some children with autism show little desire to interact with children or adults. Children without early parent relationships – such as some Romanian children adopted into homes in Great Britain (see Rutter and O'Connor 2004) – often had poor peer relationships as they grew. In general, though, the majority of children are keen to interact with other children and this interest motivates them to seek those social others.

Self-Regulation

Recall that self-regulation begins early in children's development. Infants respond with a decrease in upset or an increase in interest early on when caregivers tend to them. From infancy to age two, caregivers' expectations for young children's behavior include learning to focus on one activity for short periods of time or to wait for a desired object, for example. Such expectations help young children to develop their self-regulation skills that will assist them when they interact with other children or attend school. For example, the same preschool girl who can attend to a reading of an entire children's book without fidgeting at home can often do the same in a school setting. Preschool children can consider how to feel and behave differently than their present state, generate positive emotions when negative experiences occur, and regulate aggression (see Cole, Martin, and Dennis 2004). Regulating emotion is a complex skill, but researchers believe that preschool age children should have a great deal of mastery at an early age.

Aggression Control

Young children must learn that their needs do not always come first and that hurting others is socially unacceptable. "Instrumental aggression" is a phrase that refers to behaviors such as the grabbing of a toy from another child. The grabber simply wants to play with that toy now! No physical harm is likely intended, yet this constitutes a form of aggressive behavior nonetheless. "Physical aggression" refers to the hitting, slapping, shoving, or pushing of another child for an intended outcome. How well thought out these outcomes are in very young children is sometimes difficult to discern. However, when children exhibit these behaviors, they need social coaching from adult caregivers so that the children develop getting along well with others as their predominant mode of interaction. By the time young children reach a formal school experience like kindergarten, both instrumental and physical aggression should be almost nonexistent for social acceptance to occur.

Perspective-Taking

About thirty years ago psychologists believed that preschool children could not distinguish between different people's views or needs and their own. We now know that children from about age four do discern differences between people and can often shift their own behavior to accommodate the social other (see Shatz and Gelman 1973).

The example in chapter 2 about young children shifting their verbal communication to accommodate the listener is a great one. This tells us that their words and tone change dependent on whether they are speaking to a younger child or to an adult; they are able to shift their perspective. How marvelous! The development of even greater perspective-taking skill continues into adulthood. It is in the adolescent period that children become more self-conscious about their views being similar to or different from their social others. Adolescents examine their own views in comparison to others daily. This is wonderful perspective-taking practice that will help them to become functioning adults with good Ph as well.

Fairness

Preschool children are able to behave in ways that signal a sense of fairness (e.g., share toys and employ turn-taking) to get along with their peers. A "sense" of fairness is somewhat difficult to attribute to one age group or understand just when this develops in children. However, the concept of induction means that adults who require young children to follow rules while explaining the need for fairness will assist them in developing a sense of fairness. For example, childcare workers who explain how sharing and taking turns help everyone in the class to get along is a good tool for instilling a sense of fairness and equity in young children.

Emotional Understanding

Children who develop positive relationships with peers have good skill at noting the emotions of others and themselves (see Saarni 1999). When a young child sees that another child is crying and asks, "Are you sad?" that child has noted the emotions of a social other, labeled it, and responded with caring. Such emotional understanding skill aids all children to feel connected to others and assists their interpretations of social events.

Positive Self-Perception

Children who have a positive perception of the self believe they have value to others and can get things done. Those children who believe they have some control over their environment are said to have "agency." Agency is simply a belief that what we do matters and we can act upon our social world for desired outcomes. Such a positive view of the self is quite global in nature, but there are domains of development in which children feel more competent than others. For example, children in elementary school can have positive perceptions about their cognitive abilities but be less certain about their social abilities. While these often go hand in hand, Susan Harter (1989) has found that children's self-perceptions can differ across domains. However, a global positive self-perception is a wonderful asset for children as they develop peer acceptance.

Imagine the preschool girl who tends toward shyness as she enters the school environment. As young children pair up to work and play, she may need some gentle encouragement from her adult caregivers and teachers about her positive assets to help her take a chance and invite a child to play with her. "Can I play with you?" or "Will you play with me?" may be two of the toughest questions young children must learn. Those children who invite other children to play often have positive self-perceptions as they interact with their peers. A positive self-perception that includes feelings of agency and worth helps children approach others with relational competence.

Social Responsivity

This construct refers to a child's noting the emotional and verbal feedback of others and responding appropriately to facilitate cooperation. Children need assets such as kindness and a willingness to offer suggestions for play with some social knowledge that others' needs are as important as one's own. For example, a preschool girl may state that she wants to play with trains but notices her peer's response is a grimace. She asks, "Don't you want to play with trains?" Noting and responding to the feedback from the social other is necessary to keep communication possibilities and peer activities going.

Behavioral Flexibility

Children who are socially savvy about others' emotions and needs can develop skills that include behavioral flexibility. A willingness to shift to an activity or behavior that others prefer is one form of behavioral flexibility. The preschool girl who invited her peer to play with trains and got a grimace may next ask, "What would you like to play?" The preschool child who can shift easily to another play activity is displaying a maturity not usually seen in younger children. Behavioral flexibility can also refer to a child's response to adult requests to change a behavior. For example, when kindergarten teachers say, "Alright, Class, put your number book away and take out your letter book," they expect that most of the class can accomplish this shift without a lot of coaching. For those children who have had a positive preschool experience, this flexibility is often evident. However, dependent on other assets such as length of focus or attention to others, some children may not have behavioral flexibility when they enter their early elementary years and they will need assistance with this skill. The ability to shift behaviors is very much needed for positive relationships and success in social environments outside the home.

Social Problem-Solving

Children who have the skills needed for peer acceptance also must engage in problem-solving. Recall the discussion in chapter 4 about how problem-solving is often needed in families as well. The complexity of human interactions means that working through conflict for the good outcomes of the self and others can be difficult at times. Often, mediation or problem-solving help to lessen the difficulties. Problem-solving is a very complex skill, but note that the prior items on our list of social skills are needed building blocks of this last item. In brief, children who can identify a problem, brainstorm solutions, negotiate with their peers, design a plan and act upon it, and reconsider their own ideas and plans with their peers are very skilled indeed. Look at this example of one adult teaching a child about problem-solving:

> Two four-year-old girls are playing at one child's house. The two argue about how to play together, trains vs. teacups, and their words become dramatic with frustration and anger. The host child announces, "I don't even have a tea set!" The guest child stands up indignantly and announces she will go home and get her tea set, exits in a flurry, slamming the door. The host mom hears the door

and eases into the situation. She says to her child, "What happened?" and gently gets the whole story of her own child wishing to play with trains while the guest child wanted to play tea party. The mom gently coaches her child through a few questions, including "How do you feel about what just happened? How do you think your friend felt? Would you like to make amends and be friends again? What could you do differently next time to avoid this kind of exit?" The young child works through the suggestions with her mom, calms herself and agrees that a tea party might work. Happily, the guest child returns with her toys and assumes a tea party will ensue. She's right, for the host child's mom has worked with her daughter to help her learn about emotions, self-regulation, perspective-taking, and negotiation. When the guest child re-enters the scene, the host child says warmly, "Let's play tea party now and maybe later they can all take a train ride!" to which the guest child agrees.

Such early attempts at negotiation and social problem-solving are needed for children to learn these skills for life. Adults who assist in this regard are helping children to be able to navigate other social situations in even more complex environments like that of childcare and school. As mentioned in chapter 3, the children who have good cognitive and social skills when they enter a classroom setting are those children who will be the most sought as playmates and friends as the children grow. Although the meaningfulness of early social skills may be obvious by now, some children have great difficulty developing peer relationships. Those children whose social worlds are bleak because of isolation are important to examine as well.

Social Isolation

Unfortunately, approximately 15 percent of our child population experience some form of social isolation with their peers. Whether through neglect or rejection these children are at risk for other poor outcomes if they do not develop more social competence. Children who lack social competence report higher dissatisfaction in other areas of development (Bierman 2004). They feel negatively about themselves, often report feelings of anger and frustration, and remove themselves from their peer groups by means of "self-imposed" social isolation. Note that I put the term "self-imposed" in quotes because of the difficulty in discerning at what point children remove themselves from possible ridicule or social failure and where their peers reject or neglect them. It is very difficult for researchers to say where and when the socially isolated child becomes so, but we know that it makes life tough for these children. For example, the children who lack social competence are more likely than their socially competent peers to have difficulty in the classroom and with controlling aggression; they may even lack the skills necessary to develop fully as adults in intimate relationships. For children who lack social skill, a kind of downward spiral can be set in motion that includes negative self-esteem, a sense of helplessness and despair, and a thwarting of development across the lifespan.

Recall that the nature of social competence is dynamic; contexts change along with the people in them. Social interaction is reciprocal and peers' responses to children can be more about the peers than the identified child who seems to lack social skill. Social others respond to any "difference" in an identified child. For example, some children who are poor may lack cleanliness or the most popular dress of the day. Other children lack physical attractiveness or have a disabling condition that makes their peer interactions more difficult. The majority of adults hope to rear children in their care with kindness and sensitivity, yet all children are not egalitarian and open to other children who appear different. Children with disabilities are at increased risk for peer rejection (Bierman 2004).

A wide variety of disabling conditions exists among children. In the United States about 10 percent of children in public schools receive education assistance because of a disability. Children may lack communication skill that would assist their signaling of interest in others. A physical disability might mean restricted movement for play and interaction. Difficulty with focus or medical conditions that require constant monitoring may be present in children. For children who deal with a disabling condition in school, social competence development can be at risk. With the advancement of laws regulating the inclusion of children with disabilities in public schools comes another task for adults responsible for these children's welfare, assistance with social competence. With the help of specially trained professionals, children can be in a school environment that is the least restrictive for their development. The development of social competence among peers and a smaller circle of friends are absolutely possible for children with disabilities with the help of adults in their lives.

Children who fall within the normal range of development on markers such as physical and cognitive ability can still have difficulties with peers. Because most children wish to be around others, behavioral, cognitive, and emotional development can be compromised by a lack of interest from our social others. Caring teachers and parents may be at a loss to determine just how to begin to help a child in this category of woe.

For shy children and for those with other social competence difficulties, interventions exist to assist them. While no panacea is available, much research has provided a strong basis for the use of social competence interventions (Bierman 2004). These interventions include the positive building of cognitive, emotional, and behavioral skill that children need in order to be socially competent. Rules about contexts and scripts or what is expected in various social settings are all a part of the process of social interaction.

Karen Bierman, a psychologist who is expert on neglected and rejected children, states that these interventions must be used with the rejected or neglected children's social partners as well. Bierman has found with her research that children differ due to their presenting difficulties with their peers. For example, children who are seen as oppositional or disruptive will require different sets of skill development than children who are painfully shy. Bierman goes on to say that when teaching children new skills, the skills should be taught separately but eventually mastered as a skill set of behaviors to be practiced with peers as the children gain skill and confidence. Let us examine one such intervention that Bierman and her colleagues have developed (see Bierman 2004).

For oppositional children, Bierman and her research group teach them to "stop and think," "say the problem and how you feel," and then teach them negotiation they call "make a deal." The children also learn to integrate these three steps and practice the skills with their peers. Such interventions have been designed and many, like these from Bierman's research group, have solid data to support their use. However, the extent to which this kind of intervention is available to children is not well known. Perhaps as we learn more about the importance of children's social skill development we will encourage the use of these interventions. Adults in such settings as childcare, preschool, and formal schooling environments, as well as in our homes, can provide social skill development opportunities to children with the hope of building not only a more effective classroom experience but also more effective people. Children who get along well with their peers are those children who develop friendships that will serve them throughout their lives. Think of friendship groups as another level of social skill young children need to develop fully. Perhaps the friendship groups will change, but the commitment to kindness, loyalty, and trust is carried with us into each new friendship possibility.

Friendship

We know that preschool children need certain skills in order to get along with their peers and that these skills assist other important development. However, it is during the elementary school years that children must develop into skilled relationship partners. By the time the elementary years arrive, children are aware that peers can be a source of fun as well as support to help them through the day. Having a peer to engage with in activities or sit with at lunch can feel like a tremendous gift to children, even in the early elementary years. Because friendships are inherently reciprocal, friendship is also a gift we give ourselves, and one that adults can help facilitate in children.

Friendship beginnings start with people in the home, siblings as well as parents. Even children as young as 12 months recognize when siblings are absent and respond emotionally. Between 12 and 24 months children derive great pleasure from older siblings and can even have bonds that no other person in the house can substitute for. While we know that sibling relationships include both positive and negative characteristics, these early bonds with siblings are thought to provide glimpses of how the children will interact with others outside of the home. When children experience pleasure in the form of fun or comfort with siblings they have another model of relationships that will help them develop friendships (see Dunn 2004).

Similar to the research data about young children and their siblings, very young children can also develop relationships with unrelated others to the extent that when the friend is not present, the child becomes lethargic and/or fussy. Look at this example:

Two girls attend the same preschool at age four. They finish each other's sentences and songs. They laugh, pretend play, and share some rowdy behavior as well. "Let's roll under the swing set and see what happens!" "OK!" By kindergarten the two have a bit of a reputation that they negatively influence each other. Their two mothers are told that they will be separated for their kindergarten classes. The girls are separated and both respond in ways that many adults would not predict. They are lethargic and seem to only enjoy the outside play period that includes their friend. Their attention lapses in the classroom and their general activity level is stifled. Two weeks into the school year the mothers confer. Both girls are having the same difficulty of adjusting to their school day without their friend, despite the mothers' efforts to get them together after school and on the weekends. The mothers, one a pediatrician and one a psychologist, go to the school and with a fair amount of determination discuss the plight of their two daughters. The pediatrician exclaims, "This is a psychiatric necessity!" The school officials agree and place the two friends back together in their classroom. The girls blossom once again. Their proximity to their friend assists their energy and their cognitive development as well as their emotional ease.

Children can develop very meaningful friendships at a young age. Their positive feelings about the self, their cognitive and behavioral development, may be facilitated or stymied depending on their friendships. Just as in the peer literature, the development of friendships is an integral part of growing up with good Ph. The foundation that the parent-child, sibling-sibling, and peer relationship practice brings sets children forth on their quest for meaningful relationships outside the home.

The nature of research in this area is correlational, however. Recall that such research results mean that when one variable differs, the other differs at about the same rate. What does this mean as we examine the socially skilled child and her friendships and later outcomes? Friendships vary with family contexts, geography, sex, ethnicity, etc. We cannot draw a straight path of causality from early positive relationships to later healthy friendships. However, what we know is that children who have solid, positive friendships also often have positive relationships with parents, siblings, and peers.

Does this relationship between relationships always work? No. Some children from one household will have great social skill with others they enjoy. Other children from the same household with ostensibly the same parent and sibling beginnings will emerge with social difficulties with peers. The complexities of family relationships and even early temperament of each child likely contribute to these varied outcomes.

Some psychologists, such as Judy Dunn in her book *Children's Friendships* (2004), state that we are just beginning to examine the pathways by which friendships develop. Differences between siblings from one home are just the tip of the iceberg when it comes to understanding the complexities of human relationships. Dunn also has a neat caveat for those interested in this area or who have the responsibility of helping the children in their care to develop social competence.

Adults do not have to take sole responsibility for friendships such that minor difficulties with peers or friendship development serves as a guilt-inducing problem for adults. Many factors can impede children's development of friendships and many can be ameliorated with encouragement from adults. However, adults who are concerned about children with seemingly serious difficulty with their peers should seek help. For parents, teachers can be a welcome resource. For teachers, parents or supervisors can often assist. Professionals who work in childcare agencies or family support centers that exist in different forms in some communities can assist concerned adults. Not all families have the means or the assertiveness that the pediatrician and psychologist had in the example of the kindergarten girls who were separated. Many families may see minor difficulties and not know how to proceed. Collaborations between adults can often assist children with minor peer difficulties to get back on a more positive path with social others. These collaborations can ameliorate a minor difficulty such that serious social deficit does not develop.

Adult Facilitation of Children's Friendships

Important adults in children's lives can exert positive influence on children's social competence and interactions with peers. Both teachers and parents teach children negotiation, how to resist peer pressure, how to be assertive without aggression, etc. The development of these very important skills relies on positive relationships between children and adults. Adults also promote friendship development and even impart a variety of messages about the importance of friendships. Further, adults who monitor and filter children's relationships provide feedback that aid children along their friendship path. Let us look at a few suggestions for such monitoring, filtering, and provision of feedback:

1 Know who the children's friends are.
2 Know the friends' parents.
3 Know where the children are at any given time of the day or night.
4 Assist with activities for the children.
5 Monitor the activities.
6 Filter the friendships.
7 Provide feedback to the children.

These few, seemingly simple suggestions can be difficult at times to manage. Children often have multiple opportunities for developing friendships in many different contexts (e.g., school, religious environments, athletic teams, etc.). However, adults responsible for children must know their friends to the extent that their behaviors and general competence are noted. A good way to gain this knowledge is by means of the second suggestion: know the friends' parents. Friends' parents who wish to know their child's friends and their parents are very likely concerned about rearing happy, competent children.

The third suggestion concerns parents who know where their children are. Literally, the whereabouts of children under adults' care or on their own is an important concern that requires a constancy in monitoring. Safety and health require this of adults as well as the psychological health of the children. The fourth suggestion concerns adults' facilitation of children's friendship activities in the home or larger contexts. This behavior on the adults' part helps pave the way for the development of solid friendships for children under their tutelage. For those parents who must work at several jobs or monitor many children, invitations that are not extended often but are well planned can be just as inviting to children as an everyday after-school play time at a host child's home. As with children, adults must monitor their own behavior and try to achieve reciprocity with engagement in activities with their children and their friends. Simply put, children's parents should give and receive invitations for their children to interact with others. While this reciprocity is not always easy, it is important to be aware of it. Let's look at two examples of how families manage this responsibility to assist their children's friendships and reciprocity.

The middle-class parents of an eight-year-old girl often have her best friend over for fishing, swimming, and general fun at their house on the bay. They know that the best friend's parents are low-income, hard-working people who have raised a great child. One day, the best friend's dad comes to pick up his child and tells the host parents how much he appreciates all of the wonderful activities they provide his child. His heartfelt gratitude is said with quiet dignity and he then issues this invitation, "Can your daughter join us for our family get together this Sunday? We start with church then the whole family eats good food and spends the rest of the day together." What a treat for both children! The bay house family agrees and both children see how loving parents can provide in different ways for their children. They have also provided a wonderful model of reciprocity.

Compare this next example to the loving example noted above:

Two sixth grade girls have become fast friends at school. One child, Colleen, runs to the car with her friend at the end of the school week and says to her mom, "Can Sarah spend the night?" Colleen's mom agrees and tells the girls they must reach Sarah's mom to make sure all of their plans are agreeable to her. Sarah's mom is tough to reach, yet Sarah assures Colleen and her mom that all will be well. Colleen's mom wishes to introduce herself to Sarah's mom and get to know her a little bit so that she will be comfortable, knowing where her child is and with whom. Colleen's mom takes both girls to her house and continues to try and reach Sarah's mom. Colleen's mom realizes that she has likely made a mistake in allowing Sarah to come to their home without her mom's permission, but she perseveres in trying to reach her. Even with the convenience of cell phones, Sarah's mom does not return any phone calls until 8 p.m. At this point, Sarah's mom acts as if she has no problem with the girls' plans. Even with an invitation to come by and visit their home, Sarah's mom declines. Rather, she tells Colleen's mom that whenever she can drop off her child the next day will be fine with her.

Look at the differences in the two friendship vignettes. In the first, both sets of parents care about their children and try to bring joy to the children, albeit in different ways. In the second, the good intentions of Colleen's mom turn out badly in that her child has begun a friendship with a child whose parent is not concerned about her whereabouts, who she is with, nor how she can assist the girls in developing their friendship. It is quite possible that Sarah's mom has several impending responsibilities that cannot be ignored and that she knows Sarah's competence is high. However, Sarah's mom's refusal to engage in any sort of information exchange beyond loose instructions for a drop off the next day should give Colleen's mom pause the next time Colleen wishes to interact with Sarah at either of the children's homes.

This is a good cue for Colleen's mom to engage in monitoring and filtering the developing friendship (suggestions five and six, above). Gentle statements such as, "I'm worried that because Sarah's mom may not know where she is or who she is with, that you may not be supervised by an adult at her house. Let me talk with Sarah's mom before you plan to go to her house." Alternatively, if Colleen wishes to invite Sarah over again, Colleen's mom could say, "Let me talk with Sarah's mom before you invite her. I was very uncomfortable that Sarah was at our house a long time before her mom returned our calls." Sadly, often children with uninvolved or overwhelmed parents cannot even get them to engage in interactions with other parents. If they do, they may be disgruntled or show more lack of regard for their children's wellbeing. Again, although most parents do not intentionally ignore their children, red flags in the form of a lack of regard should be attended to by parents who do care about their children's overall development, including friendships.

While I am not suggesting that every interaction between children must be monitored or filtered, some degree of both assists children in their healthy development. Monitoring and filtering children's friendships can be narrow or broad, dependent on the contexts and developmental levels of the children. However, when parents and teachers monitor developing and dissolving friendships, they can assist children with their complex social world. As always, when the children get older than the elementary years and become more mobile and independent, such monitoring can be difficult. Whatever amount of monitoring and filtering adults can muster, practice it! Use the seven suggestions for keeping track of children's social worlds. The seventh suggestion about providing feedback to children should be accomplished with each of the other suggestions. That is, parents should tell children of their interest in their friends, their values and behaviors, that they would like to assist them with getting together with friends and supporting their positive interactions. Such commentary provides children with important information about the adults' interest in their welfare, as well as other children's welfare. During the adolescent period of development, many of the children in this age group will forcefully denounce such monitoring/filtering intervention as demeaning or ridiculous. Adolescents present some new problems or perhaps the same issues with different possibilities.

Adolescents' Friendships

Adolescents are quite mobile and many desire greater autonomy from parents than in their younger years. By the time children reach their adolescent period, they are very likely going to school early, staying late, engaging in athletics or fine arts, and making new friends in new places every week. To be with friends they can walk, bicycle, be transported by adults, and by age sixteen in most states, drive vehicles themselves. For much of the child's day, parents may not know all of the adolescents' peers. For adults responsible for adolescents, the seven suggestions for tracking friendships still apply. However, dependent on the autonomy values present in a family, various degrees of independence may be allowed that influence the use of the suggestions for assisting children with friendships. For example, some families may allow their adolescents with driver's licenses to travel to any desired destination without adult supervision and without knowing the peer or friendship group who will share the adventure. Other families will not allow their licensed adolescents to drive independently without knowing exactly who is expected to travel with the child and their destination.

Of course, any combination of agreement between parents and children is possible, including the fact that adolescents will push on boundaries to a great extent such that information about friends they are engaging with has no basis in reality. The adolescents may not be telling the truth, or the whole truth (e.g., picking up five friends instead of two). The point is simply to know as much as possible with the family's values intact. Of course, I would argue that the first example above of a driving teen without parental supervision or monitoring is a big mistake. Knowing children's maturity levels, vulnerability to risky behaviors, etc., helps adults decide how much autonomy to grant to their children at any age. Using the seven suggestions for monitoring children's friendships will assist adults throughout the children's development. Such monitoring and filtering by adults help children stay on that good Ph path. Just how families decide the limits of an adolescents' autonomy can vary a great deal dependent on family backgrounds and values.

Autonomy and Peer Influence

In the United States a very strong, white, middle-class norm exists that children begin to sever parental bonds and accept large amounts of responsibility for themselves when they reach the late adolescent period. Although this age of responsibility has been increasing with the rise of college education attendance and a delay in economic independence in the last three decades, it is still the case that an assumption about adolescent autonomy concerning their daily decision-making remains quite strong. One example of how strong this message is concerns the extent to which peer influence is thought to be prominent in adolescence.

Peers are often discussed negatively in popular media as though these "bad" children take over other children; their persuasive techniques to corrupt the "good" children must be thwarted daily. Peer influence during the early and late adolescent years is quite strong and some of it is negative. However, researchers who have examined peer and parental influence find that parental influence is often as strong as peer influence and in fact, adolescents choose friends whose values match those taught by their parents. Further, the influence of peers and friends in adolescence can be quite positive (see Santrock 2007). However, adults responsible for adolescents should no more abdicate their influencing role about peers than in the early childhood years. How each family decides to lessen control and grant more autonomy to children with their peers will vary.

While many adults agree that friendships are important to children, not all cultures or families place the same value on friendships as white, middle-income families in the United States. Concepts such as autonomy from family and closeness with peers are not supported universally. Adolescents in different cultures of the world and from diverse ethnic backgrounds in the United States are granted autonomy at varying rates (see Santrock 2007). In some cultures obedience to parental authority is strong and can be seen in such behaviors as the selection of a spouse by the adults for the adolescents. In the United States, Asian-American adolescents' adherence to parental authority is often greater than that of Euro-American adolescents. The extent of autonomy granted by some Asian-American parents is related to whether the family or collective is enhanced by such granting of independence. For example, some Asian-American parents may be delighted about friendships that include study groups. Such friendships can promote the success of the adolescents in the school environment and bring honor to the family. Similarly, Latino families often promote a collectivist value.

For Latino families, respect for elders and proper conduct is expected so strongly that two Spanish words for this adherence are used to describe this value: *familismo* and *respeto* (Triandis 1994). The family is central to behavior (*familismo*) and proper behavior (*respeto*) regarding every relationship is expected. There is some evidence that as Latino families acculturate or take on the white Western norms of the middle class in the United States, these values may decrease in importance to the family. Nonetheless, in many Latino families this collectivist value, or emphasis on the family, is strong and helps parents guide their children. While Latino families are happy their children have friends, many believe that friendships should not detract from family relationships and responsibilities. These families' rules about autonomy often vary from the individualistic values of white middle-class families in the United States.

One caveat that is important to remember concerns the fact that families from any ethnic background can differ from the average family in that ethnicity category. Expecting homogeneity, or a lack of variability because of one factor such as ethnic origin, only serves to stigmatize or categorize families in ways that do not promote understanding of all people. For example, the term "Latino" refers to people whose origins are in the Spanish-speaking Caribbean, Mexico, and Central and South America. Much diversity exists among these peoples, despite some commonality of origin. While research is lacking concerning Latino families' views about friendships, differences in history, country of origin, socioeconomic status, and acculturation in the United States are all likely related to the value each family places upon friendships.

Social Competence as Pathway

The social competence of children is one pathway on their good Ph journey. Their abilities to seek and interact well with social others are indicators of their overall development and later success as adults. Practice with loyalty and commitment in friendships helps children with their own growth and maturity concerning partnering relationships that will follow in adolescence and young adulthood. The psychological health of children is very dependent on their relationships in general, including their interactions in social domains outside of the home. Peers and friends give children information about themselves and the world. Moreover, the family bonds are not usurped by these relationships, but rather serve to act as monitors and filters for children's friendships. Peer and family values are often congruent and act in concert as children develop. In chapter 6 we will examine how family values are transmitted through words and rituals and how these generational patterns can be growth inhibiting or growth promoting for children.

Chapter 6

Well-Armed: Transmitting Values to Children

◆ ◆ ◆

The battle scene is a bright, stimulating sight-and-sound cacophony aimed at the mind and spirit of the Soda Pop Kids. The child warriors look determined but small in the overwhelming environment.

Commander Light Wars barks to his troops: "Values shields to the ready! Deflect! Repel! Dissolve! Disengage!"

A noisy, clanging, smoky battle scene can be discerned by the sleeping parent. He awakens in a cold sweat and shakes his head at the humor he can find in his "nightmare."

He knows where his adolescents are, safe in their beds. He knows he and other caring people have assisted them with learning a set of values that can serve them well, especially important in these years of newly forming independence of thought and action. The father says to himself, "Values shields in place, hope they come in handy!"

The fifth measure for good Ph concerns the extent to which children are armed with values, congruent with the lives they are expected to lead. Adults who are responsible for children teach them how to behave toward one another, how to achieve and persevere despite the possibility of adversity, and how to keep themselves intact physically and psychologically. The battle metaphor in the title of this chapter and as the theme in this vignette seems appropriate; stimulating people, events and contexts that bombard children, must be filtered or battled from time to time. Although the father in the vignette cannot be certain his children use the values they have learned from him each day, he can feel assured that he and other caring people have taught them well. These social relationships prove once again to be integral to the healthy psychological development of children. Good Ph in this chapter means teaching children important values to give them a basis for their development throughout the lifespan.

The Commander's name "Light Wars" in the vignette is an allusion to the role of values as a beacon when children face tough decisions about their behavior. These values serve as a guide, a place to begin when children encounter difficult, sometimes murky problems. Boundaries and expectations for behavior taught with warmth can shield children from negative influences, but only so far as they will use them. As children learn about those aspects of life that caring adults value, they become better able to weigh important information concerning their own development. Recall from chapter 4 that a part of family belongingness includes helping children see their responsibility to others and to themselves, and to be actively engaged in learning independent decision-making. Clear values transmitted with warmth from one generation to the next assist in children's decision-making. Parental socialization of values to children is one important focus of this chapter. However, there is a dynamism and reciprocity within the parent-child unit that has also been studied. Dynamism refers to the process of values transmission and aspects of the receiver or child; children accept or reject others' values. These interactions are reciprocal in that children also transmit their values to parents and others.

In this chapter we will examine the reciprocal nature of values socialization. While data concerning the transmission of values from children to their parents are scarce, it is of interest nonetheless. Children and their parents socialize each other and children's responses to their parents' values are an important part of the values socialization interactions, while peers also play an important role in the socialization of children's values. We will examine research concerning the degree of congruence between peer and parent values.

The importance of contexts and family backgrounds relevant to the transmission of values and their use will be examined as well. The existing data about parental socialization and modeling of values have a decidedly middle-class, European-American research base. Throughout the chapter, multicultural data will be discussed concerning values and diverse people when they are available. The complexities of interpreting research about values transmission with people of diverse backgrounds is another important aspect of this discussion.

I used the term "inoculation" in chapter 4 to describe how children's decision-making that is facilitated by reasonable adults in safe environments is good practice for the adolescent years. Decisions concerning their physical and psychological health can be made with the family's values in mind. Parental values transmission has a significant database in psychology. However, while the discussion about the impact of important non-parental adults is less well established, there are researchers who emphasize their role in children's lives as well.

Teachers and religious and community leaders provide modeling as well as direct teaching about how children can develop into people who have a value-based core that helps insure their own health and that of others. We will examine some research about the concept of competent adults who act as mentors and provide values transmission in environments external to the home.

We will examine how adults instruct and model standards of right and wrong and how these standards assist in relationships and in facilitating a productive life. Recall that both modeling and induction are powerful tools with which to teach children. Two areas of values transmission will be examined in this chapter: autonomy and educational achievement.

Values Are Us

People are often judged by the set of values they use to live their lives. What is meant by the term "values?" Most people can likely generate a definition and perhaps a few examples of values that they find worthy of transmitting from one generation to the next. The definition of a value for this book is simply this: "Any attitude or behavior that is thought to be growth promoting for the self and others, an exemplar or standard of conduct." It is very much like a life script. Values help people decide how to lead a productive life. Adults who are cognizant of the values that assist them in their decision-making are better able to be mentors and teachers to the children in their lives. What do adults value? Let us examine a list of possibilities before detailing research concerning two areas of values transmission: autonomy and educational achievement.

What do we value?
1   Consideration of others
2   Achievement
3   Autonomy
4   Tradition
5   Religiosity
6   Security (safety of self and others)

Are you still generating your own list of values? Excellent! People differ in their values from family to family, country to country, and on an individual basis. People hold values because of many factors, such as parental influence, and these influences are often associated with factors that psychologists call "demographic." Demographic information refers to people's country of origin, both historic in generations past and present-day, their socioeconomic status (SES) – that is, earnings and economic level attained – their education, biological sex, and age group, including historical cohorts. "Historical cohorts" refer to those people who experience the same patterns of events because of their date of birth. For example, adults in the United States who experienced the Viet Nam War either as soldiers or observers share that historical period with all other people in their age group. This Viet Nam cohort group may have developed values that include, for example, an urgent sense of helping others on an international level or the importance of freedom to criticize the government in a democracy.

A myriad of factors influence people's values. For ease of comparison to the list of values generated previously, compare the factors below to the values list:

Factors related to values
1   Family factors, including parental style and education.
2   Demographics, present country of origin and of elders, SES, educational level, biological sex, age group, and historical cohort.
3   Important social others such as kin, peers, teachers, employers.
4   Personal experience and development.

Just how these precursors or factors are related to the development of certain values over others is not well understood. One example from the research will assist in viewing this complexity. Look at the first list of possible values people hold. At number six is "security (safety of self and others.)" Now check the list concerning factors that could be associated with such a value. Look at number two on this list, which includes "demographic factors ... country of origin." Is safety a value that people in the United States are concerned with daily? Perhaps this is more so now than before the tragedies of September 11, 2001, but to an extent that most people would generate this concern as a value? It is unlikely. However, this value was examined and found to be important to youth who live in Israel by a psychologist who is an expert on family values among Israelis, Ariel Knafo (2003).

Knafo found this value ranked among the top three for Israelis parents and adolescents in her study. The historical and current context of life in Israel makes safety a practical, everyday value that guides how people live. While people in the United States today may have some anxiety about boarding an airplane for travel, Israeli citizens are cognizant of their value of safety every day. Their historical and current context demands a vigilance and prioritizing of safety over many other values.

Another example about the complexities of value formation in children may assist our understanding of parental values as factors associated with their development.

> An adolescent enters a t-shirt shop with his parents during a travel excursion. He selects a t-shirt that has a sepia-toned photograph on it of four great Native-American chiefs in the United States. The caption on the shirt reads "Homeland Security: Fighting Terrorism Since 1492." The father says to the adolescent, "Are you sure you want to buy this shirt? It might offend people." The adolescent responds, "Yes, I know what it means and I know our government was wrong in its treatment of the Native people of America." The father gives it one more attempt, "I agree with you, Son. While I believe that we are supposed to speak out when we see wrongs, teachers or other adults might view you negatively without really *knowing* you when they read the shirt." The adolescent answers that he understands the arguments but that they give him more resolve to buy the t-shirt and wear it. He buys the shirt and wears it proudly.

What values is this trio honoring? Several, likely taught in part by the two parents whose values can be seen in the father's discussion with the child:

1 Citizens should speak up publicly about wrongs by their government – freedom of speech
2 A clever twist of a phrase can bring a smile – humor has worth.
3 Arguing differing opinions with elders is allowed – induction means giving children a chance to state their position.
4 Adolescents require varying degrees of autonomy in their decision-making – autonomy is valued over the elder's view.

These four values are not held by everyone in the United States. Perhaps some families do not allow adolescents to make these kinds of decisions; arguing with a parent may be considered rude and lacking in filial obligation. Perhaps some Native Americans would see no humor in the shirt's caption and cringe at the incongruence of a photograph of their great chiefs being used in such a mercenary way. Values transmission is a complex process that psychologists have examined for only a few decades, but we do have some data that help us understand this important aspect of being responsible adults to the children in our lives.

Parental Socialization of Values

Parents give their children messages about their values daily. Through modeling, reasoning, and direct teaching children learn their parents' values. Historically in psychology it was believed that an authoritative parent or one who uses warmth and reasoning will be more likely to raise children with values congruent with their own. More complex theories about the paths through which values are transmitted exist today, but the emphasis on warmth remains very strong in the research.

Grazyna Kochanska (2002), a developmental psychologist, describes the bonds between parents and children that will promote congruence in values. Kochanska has found through her research that responsive parents who wish their children to be happy are likely to have children who espouse their values. A give-and-take that includes parents' sensitivity to children's developmental levels, moods, and behaviors, including transgressions, is thought to contribute to values congruence between parents and their children. Children who know they are loved and who are provided standards of conduct with appropriate prompting when needed respond to their parents' values and adopt them as their own, according to this research. Kochanska terms this "mutually responsive orientation." Parents are sensitive to the children's needs as they teach them values, their standards of behavior. This flexibility or dynamism inherent in such positive interaction is thought to promote values that are congruent between parents and their children.

Such a view about parents' perceptions of their children's responses to their teachings suggests a "bidirectionality" concerning values socialization. Bidirectionality simply refers to the extent to which children are not blank slates or sponges that soak up everything that is taught. Rather, bidirectionality means that children respond to adult messages concerning values, based on many factors.

According to psychologist Joan E. Grusec, an expert in values socialization, children must perceive their parents' messages about values accurately and must adopt them as their own in order for values socialization to occur. This means that parents' direct teaching and modeling of the values they wish their children to have must have a coherence or congruence of their own. The old axiom of the importance of "practicing what we preach" is relevant (see Grusec and Kuczynski 1997).

One example from chapter 5 concerned a mother's helpfulness with her child after an argument with a peer. The two young girls could not come to an agreement about what activity to engage in and the guest child exited the home, seemingly not to return. The mother took time to examine the event with her child. By her statements, questions, and tone the mother gave her child several messages about the argument and the importance of resolving conflict and the consideration of others. The mother supported her child's feelings and the guest child's feelings, thus showing how kindness is an important value. The mother asked the child to discuss what could happen next time, imparting a value of cooperation and personal responsibility. All of this discussion gave the child cues about how to conduct herself, including self-regulation and hope for the future. Fortunately for all in the example, the host child was able to act upon her mother's notes to her when the guest child returned to play again. The mother made her values clear and discussed them with warmth. The child heard her mother's values and was able to practice them very soon after the discussion.

The mother took advantage of an event in young children's lives that can occur daily. Wading our way through conflict can have meaningful outcomes if we use values of responsibility and caring. According to researchers, what else must this mother engage in to assist the transmission of her values? This mother must model the same personal responsibility and caring when she confronts difficulty and conflict in her own life. Whether it is a simple compromise with friends concerning a movie choice, or a more difficult decision with her spouse concerning the family's financial resources, when the mother models the values she espoused during the teaching moment with her daughter, she is providing another important link for her child. Her teaching and modeling are congruent.

In order for children to accept parents' values as their own, they must have clear messages given through multiple means of teaching and modeling about expected standards of living. This clarity promotes an understanding of the value, an accurate perception of the value. Incongruity of these standards can mean that children can become confused about parental values and they may have difficulty discerning what parents believe to be important. When a clear message of the expected value is given, other factors promote or inhibit the child's acceptance of the parents' values for themselves.

Grusec agrees with Kochanska: adults who give behavioral prompts about values with sensitivity to the child's point of view and developmental level transmit an environment of warmth and caring that children will respond to. Under these conditions, it is believed that children will more likely accept the values of the important adults in their lives. Children with the ability to regulate their behavior with their parents' values in mind do so because of positive interactions with these adults.

Research on Autonomy as a Value

As children grow, adults give them increasing freedom to explore their worlds and acquire new concepts and behaviors. Without some freedom to explore, basic skills like walking could not be attained, let alone the acquisition of values. Part of being human is that new experiences facilitate our development. The renowned scientist Jean Piaget described this as constructing our own development in the environment (see Gruber and Voneche 1977). Adults grant children autonomy to explore their worlds based on their knowledge about children, the world, and their own values. Different cultures have various social prescriptions about the value of autonomy, however.

Not all people hold the same values concerning autonomy and in many cultures, concern for the family or group is held in much higher esteem than individual autonomy. An examination of various cultures' values allows for a multicultural view of any phenomenon. While adolescents around the world are often given more freedom and responsibility than children, from one culture to the next, this granting of autonomy varies. For example, the age at which adolescents engage in seeking autonomy, independent of their parents' thought and actions, varies. Children who are raised in more collectivist cultures like that of Asia will seek autonomy at a later age than Euro-American children as adolescents and will likely express and maintain obligations to their parents and families well into their adult years.

Researchers have attempted to explain how many young adults uphold their parents' values and behavioral demands, even throughout the lifespan. For example, multicultural psychologist Harry C. Triandis describes how cultures in which an allegiance to family is prominent, such as India and Japan, often have parents who choose marriage partners for their adolescents. He goes on to say that a marriage to another is considered a marriage to the group and is reflective of an entire family's good judgment, success, and hope for the future. Cultures in which this strong allegiance to the group is the norm are called "collectivist." Each person has worth, but the true test of a person resides in their group allegiance and concern for others in their group. Compare this level of autonomy or subordination of individual values to parents' values to an "individualist" culture like that so prominent in the United States (see Triandis 1994).

Triandis explains that individualism is a concept that has the individual as the focus of development and is often found in cultures that are affluent, complex, and industrialized over a long period of time. People from individualist cultures have many options for their development and compete for material success. Autonomy overall is stressed and the group's wishes are subordinate to the individual's. Such is the nature of many family groups in the United States. However, Triandis cautions that assuming a monolithic character to one country, culture, or subculture is ill-advised. Even though one culture can be considered to have values that are collectivist or individualist, there can still be variation based on factors like families' countries of origin.

Acculturation of various groups to the dominant culture in the United States is one factor found to be important in the examination of autonomy values. "Acculturation" simply refers to people's process of accepting a culture's beliefs and values in which they live. For example, Triandis writes that Hispanic-origin people in the United States who are acculturated to Euro-American values tend to be more individualistic than Hispanic people who are more recent immigrants and are less acculturated. How might we apply this finding to our marriage partner example? Some adults in India or Japan may demand that their children marry partners who they choose. At one time, people of Hispanic origin in the United States may have made similar demands of their children. Today, second and third generations of families rearing their children in the United States are more likely to adopt a compromise of individualist and collectivist culture, depending on their dates of immigration or birth in the United States. It is possible that U.S. natives today with Asian or Hispanic heritage may express family obligation and concern for their children's marital partners, yet allow them to choose their own mates with much autonomy intact.

Which value is the best? No judgment of this can be made, according to Triandis. Each culture or family group makes decisions about demands for autonomy based on their own histories and what has worked for them historically. Extremes of collectivism or individualism contain seeds of peril, however, according to Triandis. Extreme collectivism may engender events such as war because of values concerning the favored group as superior to all other groups who are unworthy of life. Conversely, extreme individualism may leave vulnerable people to fend for themselves, without a collective response. These cautions seem to indicate that Triandis is an advocate for a balance of individualism and collectivism in families. Family of origin, place of origin, and multiculturalism are constructs that assist our understanding of the development of values concerning autonomy. Other factors that affect families have been found to also impact the socialization of values.

In an important study in the United States by sociologist Hong Xiao (2000), the sex of the parent, and more often mothers' values and social class, predicted parental values that are transmitted to children.

An examination of his data shows that middle-class parents value autonomy, but that working-class parents are more likely to value conformity to authority, rather than autonomy. Class differences can be understood given the amount of independence workers are thought to have, whether from white collar or blue collar employment environments.

Xiao also looked at differences between males and females concerning autonomy. Previous research on the socialization of autonomy in the United States had found that boys were given more autonomy messages than girls. That is, boys were encouraged to explore their environments independently and girls were encouraged to be nurturing or connected to others in their behavior. Xiao suggests that since the Feminist Movement of the 1970s in the United States, these messages about autonomy have begun to shift. Xiao found that middle-class women valued autonomy more than middle-class men, thus suggesting that girls and boys receive different messages today, compared to those before the turn of this century. This new finding indicates how important historical patterns can be concerning the socialization of values. Other historical changes bring new questions for the study of autonomy vs. connection to others.

The Higher Education Research Institute based at the University of California Los Angeles examines data from incoming freshmen each year in the United States. In the short space of time between 2004 and 2005, many freshmen appear to have changed in their values concerning helping others. By 2005, 67 percent of the freshmen class reported they would likely work in their communities for the betterment of others. This increase, though just 3.9 percentage points from the previous year, accounts for about 50,000 more freshmen nationally who are willing to help others than in the previous year. The authors believe that this increase may be due in part because of the world events of the Indian Ocean tsunami in 2004 and the hurricanes in the Gulf of Mexico in 2005. When the needs of others are communicated, many young people today are responding with a collectivist value in the United States (Higher Education Research Institute 2005).

Autonomy as a value is promoted by family factors such as parental emphasis, demographic variables such as place of birth, social class, and gender, and is also related to historical events that occur outside of the family. Children receive many messages about the value of autonomy. They must perceive what is important to others and through the process of their own development in various contexts that include historical events, accept or reject the values of others. Let us now turn to the socialization of the value termed "academic achievement."

Academic Achievement

Academic achievement is a fairly recognizable phrase that refers to the degree of success children have while in their school years. Researchers have found that when parents value school success, children very often adopt this value as their own.

The parental value of academic achievement may be one of the strongest values the research literature supports. Parents often list this as the most important value they transmit to their children. Further, this value predicts academic success better than any other value examined. In one study by developmental psychologist Michelle M. Englund and her colleagues (2004), maternal values concerning children's academic success in first grade predicted whether these same children attended college by age 23. These findings mean that mothers who hold a value of academic success have children who will go to college. Many researchers have also established a link between maternal education and their children's college attendance. Based on these data, a link becomes obvious between the importance of mothers' views concerning academic achievement through their spoken value and their own college attendance. Values transmission is more likely with caring teaching and modeling. Consider, once again, James Comer.

When renowned psychiatrist James Comer wrote about his journey to become an educated person, he credited the value his mother placed on academic achievement as one of the most motivating forces in his life (see Comer 2004). Comer wrote about his mother's value of academic achievement in his book, *Maggie's American Dream: The Life and Times of a Black Family*. There he recounted how his mother's vision of the life well-lived included being an educated person. Although not college educated herself, Maggie Comer instilled in her children how education could help them succeed at whatever their passions could dream. Comer went on to become the foremost authority on educational reform in the United States, as well as one of the most respected psychiatrists of his generation. Based on years of research as well as his own history, Comer understands how academic achievement must be a value that parents from all backgrounds transmit to their children.

Other researchers have been concerned with negative influences on children's academic achievement, such as economic deprivation. However, the research often credits parental valuing of education as more powerful than SES or peer support. Certainly, this was the case with the parents of James Comer, who were hard-working people but economically disadvantaged. Writing in 2005, Andrea Smith, Barry H. Schneider, and Martin D. Ruck examined adolescents who were successful in school. They found that these adolescents had parents across income groups who valued and supported their academic achievement. Thus, parental value and support were stronger predictors than either SES or perceived support from their peers. Children from economically deprived families can succeed in school when their parents place a high value on academic achievement.

We know that many parents in the United States transmit a value of academic achievement to their children. However, in an often-cited study by psychologists Harold Stevenson, Shin-Ying Lee, and their colleagues, other cultures have parents for whom academic achievement is the *strongest* value they impart to their children (see Stevenson and Lee 1990). These researchers found that mothers in China and Japan valued academic excellence more so than American mothers. The Asian mothers were more strict and demanding about academic achievement than the American mothers. While the American mothers also held a value of the importance of the cognitive growth of their children, this perspective was different than "academic achievement" as more narrowly defined by these researchers. They believe that this difference in values sheds light upon the greater success of Chinese-American and Japanese-American children at school in the United States, compared to their European-American counterparts.

The value of academic achievement transmitted from parents to children has a solid research base. Social class, biological sex, historical patterns, and patterns in a specific culture contribute to our understanding of how values are transmitted to children. However, other research supports how the values of peers and important adults outside of the home can also be positively related to school success for children. While not as well researched as the parent-child dyad, a few studies contribute to the understanding of the importance of nonparental others in the healthy development of children.

Peers

Remember our example from chapter 5 about the two friends who seemed to spell trouble for one another at their school and school officials separated them? The girls were much happier and attentive when they were brought back together. Such is the positive nature of important social relationships that are external to the home. As children grow, the values of peers are related to the values children accept as their own. It is thought that peer influence peaks around ages fourteen to fifteen for children and begins to decline by the time they reach age eighteen. While many adults bemoan the influence peers have on each other, peers help children negotiate a social world with less hierarchy than that they must traverse with adults. Research concerning peer vs. parental values has taken a surprising turn in recent years: parent and peer values are often congruent.

The popular belief in the United States that peer influence is mostly negative is just not supported by data. Rather, what psychologists find is that competent parents structure their children's lives such that peer and friendship choices are facilitated by the parents. Parents who monitor and filter their children's friendships, as discussed in chapter 5, increase their chances of seeing congruence between their values, their children's values, and the children's peers' values. Psychologist Ariel Knafo (2003) even found that parents choose their children's schools, based on their own values. For example, those parents with more traditional religious values are more likely to choose traditional religious schools for their children. Obviously, as many parents engage in this behavior, they are formally impacting the school contexts of their children by their choices. Other parents who wish their children to be in a traditional environment choose the same school.

Parent and peer values are often congruent throughout children's lives. While adolescents may engage in conformity with their peers concerning issues such as mode of dress, core values such as concern for others or academic achievement are often held by the adolescents' friendship groups as well. Peer influences can be positive or negative, but the sound values base transmitted by parents to their children is often seen among these children's peers as well. Children choose to affiliate with other children who are similar to them when they are young; parental guidance affects these choices as well. Although some experimentation can be found during the adolescent years, it is still the case more often that similar adolescents find each other and form friendship groups that honor many of the core values taught at home.

Peers may influence children with their values concerning such issues as mode of dress or appearance, even to the extent that parents can be uncomfortable. Children who are beginning to value autonomy from adults, yet are influenced by peers, may desire "fitting in." Long hair for boys or torn jeans may be an expression of autonomy from adults. However, such influence is not likely to impact children negatively. With core values in place, these "experiments" are considered normal and have merit in that some freedoms for children can assist their learning about the world. For example, when adolescents decide to seek employment, they may encounter potential employers who say very clearly, "If you work here, you must be neat. No long hair and no torn jeans are allowed." At this point, the adolescent can examine to what extent the value of an "in style" appearance is to be upheld over the desire for employment. This balancing becomes a teaching metaphor for employment throughout the lifespan.

While we are discussing style among children, this is one area in which children are thought to influence their parents' values. In the beginning of this chapter, I noted that some reciprocal socialization of values occurs between children and parents. Modes of dress or music values can be transmitted from children to their parents. Again, while not as important to a person's life as a value such as achievement, children's focus on new ideas and popular culture can be seen in some parents' values.

Non-Parental Adults Who Influence Values

Teachers, community leaders, and extended family members can influence children's values development positively. Teachers who value academic success and have high expectations for children contribute to their success in the classroom. According to psychologists Claude M. Steele and Joshua Aronson, whole school systems must communicate the value of educational achievement through their behaviors, including that of their teachers in order for all children to be successful in school. Through laboratory experimentation and in practical educational settings, their ideas have proven effective for children of all ages. Teachers and administrators who hold a value that each child's academic success is a malleable work-in-progress have effective schools. Positive communications and expectations are transmitted to the children, who will in turn develop this value as their own. A value that includes every child's potential will translate into positive outcomes for the children, their schools, and whole communities (see Steele and Aronson 1995).

As Ariel Knafo has found, parents often choose their children's schools, based on the values transmitted there. Teachers and administrators who have values similar to the parents' instruct the children many times a week in academic curriculum as well as values transmission. Many educators propose that the very nature of the classroom in the United States imparts values of autonomy and democracy. Individual achievement is honored and each child has an equal opportunity to achieve. While we know that by virtue of economic disadvantage many children do not have positive experiences at school, when teachers and administrators value educational achievement along with parents, children value this achievement as well.

Values and the Person

Renowned psychologist Laurence Steinberg summed up the importance of values transmission and the developing child (see Steinberg 2004). As children grow, they are influenced by the important people in their lives. Their backgrounds, including their parents' styles, their own experiences and behaviors, assist them in forming their own value systems. Recall the notes at the beginning of this chapter that included information about the dynamism inherent to values transmission. The recipients of values information may either accept or reject them. While most adolescents' values look quite similar to those of their parents, they are able to use their developing cognitive and social skills to more objectively examine parental values. Adolescents' experiences give them information about the world that may differ from their parents. They are able to examine the values they were reared within and decide which values to retain as a part of themselves.

Adults responsible for the promotion of good Ph in children can take heart that many of their values will be accepted by the children they have helped rear. In the United States, autonomy and independence of thought are valued. For those adolescents who are examining their worlds and values with a kind of freshness, it is hoped that their independence also means an adoption of even greater valuing of those aspects of life that are growth promoting for all. Concern for others may increase through the years, as we have seen in the new Freshmen Class of 2005. In this culture of individualism, perhaps others' needs will promote stronger values of our interrelatedness and using power to assist others. Psychologically healthy children have aspects of individualism and collectivism in their values. They value their own achievement and helping others. Once again, we are reminded of how good Ph depends on relationships.

Chapter 7

Fun-Raising

◆ ◆ ◆

The two children are munching away on their dinners, sitting on a stoop at the newly renovated building that will house the area's women's shelter. They have worked hard as volunteers for much of the day, helping prepare for the night's fund-raising festivities. Under the supervision of caring adults, they have raked the yard, picked up trash from some new construction and overall, had a very busy day for two ten year olds. Their moods are up-beat, even though they are tired and hungry. In a moment of reflection, one of the children is overheard saying to her friend, "They should call this 'fun-raising!'"

Fun-raising, indeed! The child has enjoyed being with her friend, is proud of her work, and knows that on this day, she has made a difference. Apparently, her parents and other important adults in her life have taught her the joys of service, fellowship, and fun. The child has developed a great sense of humor and in a positive moment, makes a statement about who she is, a person with caring and humor.

The sixth measure for good Ph concerns how fun, humor, and laughter help everyone get through a busy day, or even a stressful one. A good sense of humor or a willingness to take the self less seriously from time to time helps people develop overall and build and sustain relationships that are so important for psychological health. The caring adults in children's lives assist them in building this skill so that they may draw upon more positive feelings when in normal developmental contexts, or encountering situations that bring them distress. Good Ph is linked with humor in children's lives.

Research within psychology concerning humor gained some momentum in the 1970s with the advent of interest in positive psychology. Recall that in chapter 1 we discussed positive psychology as a fairly recent movement that includes researchers and clinicians who wish to understand how people develop competence and maintain it in adverse circumstances. As topics go, humor is still a rather small body of research today, however. For example, we have some data in the adult literature about how laughter is related to the body's ability to produce endorphins or "feel good" chemicals. There exist a few studies that show, for example, how the use of humor may alleviate depressive symptoms in adults. When children are examined, the data become less available than that in the adult literature. Research that assists the understanding of the role adults play in teaching the health-promoting value of humor to children is mostly nonexistent. Fun-raising has been virtually ignored by psychologists, but the roots of the benefits of warm relationships and the modeling of fun *are* in the literature and give families and teachers ideas about how to promote fun as they help children develop. We will look at the research that has examined the links between fun and humor in adults and the development of children, as well.

In this chapter, the term "fun" will be used just as everyone understands it, an experience that brings us joy or amusement. While laughter and humor are certainly related, they are two different areas of study in the sciences. Laughter is that small chuckle or deep feeling in our bellies that tells us and others that something has provided amusement. In laughing, people emit air and their bodies produce a movement, a sound, or both. Psychologists refer to a laugh as an "affective display." This simply means that the positive feelings are shown on our faces and sometimes in our whole bodies. Although every culture has its own rules about how much laughter is allowed in public and private contexts, every group of people on the earth laughs.

"Humor" as a related area of study to laughter can be described as an experience that has raised arousal or tension with some sort of incongruity that is worthy of a second look. The second look or pause leads people to attempt to resolve the incongruity and enjoy the moment as amusing. Humans must enjoy the opportunity to engage in this bit of "mental gymnastics" because when such a discrepancy between an expectation and the reality is given in a non-threatening atmosphere, we are amused! The child in the opening vignette to this chapter was aware that much hard work was behind her. She felt good about herself and had fun assisting adults to raise funds for people less fortunate than she. A turn of phrase helped her describe the incongruity she must have been experiencing: her hard work with fund-raising felt like fun to her, an irony she enjoyed. The use of irony has been discussed for fifty years in psychology as a tool for revealing a simple curiosity or absurdity when two events or entities seem to be incongruent (see Lefcourt 2001; Martin and Lefcourt 1983). When spoken with warmth and in situations of mutual trust, ironic humor is enjoyable, as in the case of the young child who worked so hard but had fun doing it. Let us examine some of the research in this area, and its relationship to adults' and children's psychological health.

Humor Research

Psychologist Herbert M. Lefcourt is renowned for his research concerning humor and psychological health. For over thirty years he has examined humor and laughter and has some insights about how he chose this area of study. He writes:

> I described what had seemed a surprising departure from solemnity at my father's funeral. The reuniting of family members from far and wide proved to be an occasion for both mirth and goodwill. This was not at all out of disrespect for the deceased but was almost in his honor. My father had always been ready to make light of the grimmest circumstances, often with a joke or cliché that somehow would fit the occasion and cause others to take it less seriously. The humor displayed at this funeral was very much in character with the way in which he would have jested had he been there to take part. Most importantly, the relatives reveled in that good humor so that everyone left the ceremonies with better feelings toward each other. (Lefcourt 2001: 5–6)

Lefcourt goes on to give one example of irony that was spoken that day: Irv, Lefcourt's father, who had been an avid gardener, was now left for the grubs! Note that Lefcourt described his father as a person with a good sense of humor and his family as better for it. Their family relationships were strengthened with the sharing of humor that the occasion of his father's funeral provided. Lefcourt went on to say that his interest in the positive aspects of individuals' use of humor for fun and coping was piqued early in his career. From his clinical work in the 1960s, Lefcourt tried to understand what aspects of people were associated with resilience or an ability to move forward in the face of adversity. After examining constructs concerning people's ability to cope with adversity for more than a decade, Lefcourt changed his focus because of the insistence of one of his students, Carl Sordoni. Sordoni asked him to consider humor as a coping strategy and the two went on to conduct humor research and publish together. From that point, Lefcourt's research focus was humor and how its use affects people positively.

The majority of the research about humor has been conducted on adults. Lefcourt and his colleagues have examined humor and found many aspects to its value as a coping mechanism, including a sign of resilience. Lefcourt has found that people with a good sense of humor are comfortable with who they are. They have a sense of agency or positive feelings about their ability to direct their own lives and establish their place in the world. They are not flappable, even when the humor is "on them." Knowing one has been tricked with an ironic incongruity and still being able to laugh is a marker of a psychologically healthy person. This laughter signals to others that such a punctuation of communication is welcome and it is also an encouraging social response that shows consideration of relationships. Lefcourt cautions that he understands how humor may be used quite negatively against people. If it is used at their expense and to their detriment, this is termed "hostile humor." Although research exists about the negative use of humor, the focus of this chapter remains the positive uses of humor that can be experienced by adults and children as "fun-raising." Part of establishing relationships relies upon the use of humor.

Overall, humor is viewed as a positive force in peoples' lives in much of the research. In Rod A. Martin and Herbert M. Lefcourt's (1983) research with humor as a moderator of psychological health, they found that adults with a good sense of humor were better able to handle negative events and regulate their moods positively. The authors believe that these findings indicate that humor acts as a buffer to stress; adults' good Ph is enhanced because of humor in their lives. Humor signals to others that social relationships exist that are important to maintain and these are related to people's psychological health. Some research studies show how a sense of humor can be a factor related to physical health as well. For example, in several studies concerning the relationship of stress and a compromised immune response, researchers have found humor to be one of the best predictors of positive outcomes, even under stress such as cancer treatment. Look at this example from Lefcourt.

Lefcourt and his colleagues published a study in which they had taken immune system samples by taking samples of blood from participants, both before and after they listened to a humorous dialogue. The participants in the study who heard the humorous dialogue had a higher level of healthy immune system chemicals in their blood than the participants who did not hear the humorous story (see Lefcourt, Davidson-Katz, and Kueneman 1990). These findings and others like it led psychologists to believe that when people are optimistic and retain a sense of humor, they are better able to maintain their immune systems to promote the health of their bodies. What a remarkable finding of the mind-body interaction!

Laughter Research

Laughter also has a relationship with positive physical outcomes. There are historical records that show philosophers extolling the physical benefits of laughter as early as the 12th and 13th centuries. Lefcourt (2001) describes the work of an American physician at Fordham University in 1928. Dr. J. J. Walsh theorized that a person's state of mind was the best predictor of a patient's health and that laughter and health vary together. If one laughs and takes time to do so, Dr. Walsh predicted better health. However, a lack of research existed about laughter as a "medicine" for many decades in the United States until the advent of the positive psychology movement. As positive psychology grew, so did the interest in laughter as a health predictor.

By the 1980s, researchers were finding that people's physical health was related to laughter. They had data to back up these claims by virtue of studies involving heart rate and other research manipulations in the sciences. For example, laughter causes an increase in heart rate and respiration that are believed to indicate physical health. By the 1990s, with the advent of magnetic resonance imaging (MRI), researchers could more easily see a brain in its normal activity without opening the skull or performing other intrusive observations.

The brain's activity during laughter could literally be seen with an MRI, quite an advance from the earlier studies. As with all physiological responses people have, laughter's relationship to other neural and chemical reactions in the brain could be seen as connected by means of the MRI.

William F. Fry, a psychiatrist and researcher of laughter and brain chemistry, found support in his studies for the earlier arguments that laughter promotes several systems of the body (see Fry 2002). When people laugh, they also increase their heart rate, respiration, and immune function, as well as releasing endorphins, or "feel good" chemicals, in their bodies. Think of the brain as the main switching station for all of this activity. According to Fry, the brain assists people with noting and understanding ambiguity or incongruence that will be resolved and translated as humor. The brain also signals the physiological response that is laughter. Fry goes on to say that researchers are still exploring just how laughter is related to other physiological responses. For example, Fry cautions that as a scientific community, researchers still do not know if people who laugh rarely are any less healthy than those who laugh regularly. There are only a few studies that have compared such groups and they have design flaws such as the measurement of participants at one time and not across time. No longitudinal data exist to support these findings. Suffice it to say, we know that laughter's physiology can be seen on an MRI and that the brain stimulates other responses in the body that are thought to be positive and health promoting.

Laughter has psychological benefits as well. Along with the benefits of helping to build and maintain relationships, laughter can help people through stressful life events and alleviate depressive symptoms after a loss. Psychologists Dacher Keltner and George A. Bonanno, experts in the study of coping after loss, examined bereaved relatives after the death of a loved one. They found that those who could laugh at a humorous event within six months after their relatives' death were better able to cope with their loss than others who were more somber in those first few months (Keltner and Bonanno 1997). These researchers believe that the bereaved people's willingness to be engaged in a positive way with other human beings signals a readiness to go forth and to be engaged with their own lives, rather than dwell on the loss of the loved one. When the respondents in their study reported they engaged in laughter that included mouth and eye facial muscles– a sincere, big laugh – they also reported lower levels of distress than those who laughed less. Among the laughers, positive emotion and overall enjoyment were high. Keltner and Bonanno also found that the people who laughed most had better social bonds with others. The authors believe that people who can laugh are better able to maintain social relationships. These data support well the relationships between humor and laughter and healthy functioning among adults.

Just how such a propensity to see the positive aspects of situations and enjoy moments of mirth are transmitted from adults to children, and how the children develop this gift, is the topic of the next section.

Children's Development of Humor

Ann S. Masten is a psychologist who is an expert in children's resilience, as discussed in chapter 1. She has examined the development of their humor as a marker of their resilience. Writing in 1986, Masten summarized what was known at the time concerning children's development of humor and its relationship to other positive functioning. For children as young as infants, humor assists with the mother-infant bond; the earliest social relationship is enhanced with humor. A mother's nuzzle at the baby's feet or other playful antics are enjoyed by the infants as early as six months of age, their smiles and giggles evident to all. As with all adult behavior, an invitation to play serves as a model for children, even very young ones. By the time children enter preschool, researchers view humor as a socially adaptive tactic with others and have also found that children use humor for coping. A slip on the floor or a tumble on the playground may be accompanied by the child popping back up and saying with a smile, "Who did that?!" Sharing a joke and a smile is mutually reinforcing in that social interaction is enjoyable and is desired in the future. Children know very early how to use humor to assist them with their social relationships.

Masten (1986) studied the extent to which other positive behaviors or competence were related to humor in children who were aged ten to fourteen. She found that social and cognitive competence were both related to children's use of humor. Children enjoy their peers who have a good sense of humor; they are viewed as competent overall and are sought after as companions. Before children can use humor, however, they must be able to access certain knowledge, be able to handle it in a symbolic way, and produce either a verbal pronouncement of humor (a joke/punch line) or a laugh when appreciating another's humor. Let us examine an example from a group of pre-teen girls.

> A dad is driving six twelve-year-old girls to a soccer match when he notes that a conversation is occurring among the girls about people from Turkey. Their talk is turning toward stereotyping people from Turkey as if they were all supportive of conflict and as though the girls knew many natives of this country. The dad interrupts and asks, "Just a minute. You're venturing into stereotyping all people from Turkey. Do any of you know a person from Turkey?" The girls answer "No," but go on to explain that they were studying the history of Turkish wars in school. In trying to develop what else to say to the girls, the dad engaged them to talk more about the Turkish wars. The girls were able to describe, indeed, many wars and battles that seemed to emanate from Turkey and its conflicts with other countries. At this point, the dad had an idea. Because the date was early in the 2003 U.S.-led invasion of Iraq and just a few years after the United States and its allies entered Afghanistan, the dad says, "Well, you *do* know about many wars that Turkish governments have been involved in. They are unlike the United States, who does not engage in international conflict!" At this, the entire carload of girls erupts into laughter. A few of the girls remark about the "truth" spoken in the incongruity and the father's use of irony to allay their stereotyping.

Several learning moments have occurred between this dad, his child, and her friends. First, he wanted to quell their stereotyping of people from Turkey. After getting them to talk a bit more about how their ideas were formed, he had an idea of his own. For U.S. citizens, the first few years of the 21st century included global conflict. These children on their way to a soccer game possessed several characteristics within themselves and their environments that are necessary in order to be engaged in humor at this level.

To begin with, one caring adult paused to help them examine their views and gently pushed them to see their stereotyping with a little humor. The use of irony to help the children see the absurdity their stereotyping was leading them to proved helpful. As for the children's developmental level, they understood the facts. These twelve-year-old girls were aware that both Turkey and the United States have been engaged in conflicts. Cognitively, they were stimulated as they discussed Turkish history before they wandered into verbalizing their stereotypes about the people. The girls were enjoying their camaraderie together and sharing their knowledge. They also understood that when the dad used the term "stereotyping," they were categorizing people unfairly and to their detriment. The girls were willing to listen to the father, showing some trust, some amount of social obligation to him as he spoke, a willingness to maintain a social relationship. Their cognitive and social interest were high as the dad intervened.

At the point that the dad asks the girls to compare Turkish people to people in the United States, the girls see the irony, the incongruity of his statement about the United States, and are able to handle the material in a fairly abstract way. Their arousal is piqued and they see the ridiculous nature of their categorizing all Turkish people together because they are able to look at themselves. The dad's punch line, "unlike the United States," sets their minds spinning for a fraction of a second and they emit loud laughs as they understand the incongruity. The girls had some fairly high understanding of factual information, used the incongruity appropriately, and were able to laugh at themselves and have insight about their stereotyping, thus resolving tension inherent in the conversation. All of this was accomplished with the use of a little humor to ease into the lesson by the dad.

As Masten (1986) suggested, children who know facts and can use material abstractly are likely able to use humor in complex ways to build and maintain relationships. When Masten discussed the findings from her research, she did so with a few caveats, however. The data do not allow us to pronounce that children who use humor will be smarter or happier than others. Overall, cognitive and social competence are related to children's humor, but as for the direction of influence, researchers do not know.

Masten and her colleagues believe that positive relationships with peers and academic success are related and that humor has its place in these relationships as well. Indeed, in the 1986 study, Masten found that the children who were high in humor had teachers who thought they were competent in the classroom. Just how the children developed humor and how these data vary together are still not fully

understood, but humor is an important factor in children's development. Humor indicates that children are cognitively and socially
engaged; that, we know. Both are markers of good Ph. We also have
some data about the use of humor by parents in their role as facilita-
tors of their children's development.

Parental Transmission of Humor

As with the other measures discussed in this book to promote children's healthy psychological development, they are very reliant on the
caring adults in their lives to use humor and fun in a positive way.
Good Ph can be promoted with humor and fun. The soccer dad from
our vignette is one good example of an adult model the children can
observe and emulate. Researchers have found some links between how
parents behave with their children and the development of humor.

Eminent psychologists Jack Block and Nathan Kogan (personal
communication, January 2007) found that playfulness in parents predicted independence in boys and their use of humor. Block and Kogan
conducted a longitudinal study with children beginning at age three
as they interacted with their parents and followed these children until
they were eighteen years of age. These psychologists were interested
in how parental behaviors in early childhood would be related to
their children's development into young adulthood. The mothers and
fathers who were high in their use of playfulness and joking with the
boys at age three had boys who were independent and full of humor
at age eighteen. Boys with playful parents had good psychological
outcomes at age eighteen.

These eighteen-year-old boys, after many years of being investi-
gated by the researchers, looked as though they were the beneficiaries
of a great gift from their parents. Recall that in chapter 6 we examined cultural differences concerning prescriptions for behavior that
include individualism vs. collectivism. Block and Kogan found that
these boys indeed had developed the cultural prescription so evident
in the United States, a high value placed on individualism and independence. These mostly white, middle-class boys were independent,
indicating that the parents had done a good job of rearing their boys
according to the cultural prescription. In addition, these boys from
playful parents also had humor in their lives at a higher rate than the

boys who were raised by the less playful parents. These data support the position that parents' use of humor with their children serves as a model for children to emulate. Modeling a behavior is a very powerful teaching tool for the development of good Ph. There is data that show how parents can use humor with their disciplinary techniques, as well.

Recall that in chapter 4 we examined disciplinary techniques of parents. Parents' efforts to make clear rules about standards of behavior help their children understand their expectations. Further, recall that adults who wish children to adopt their standards of behavior must use induction to guide this along. That is, when children are encouraged to discuss parental standards of behavior with them, they are more likely to adopt the standards as their own. This kind of parental flexibility is related to maintaining warmth in parent-child relationships and the children will more likely internalize the messages from the adults. Let's review one study among the few that have examined the use of humor by parents in their disciplinary techniques that helps maintain warmth.

In 2004, Alicja Rieger published a study about parents' use of humor among families of children with disabilities (Rieger and Ryndak 2004). She examined families whose life circumstances meant that their approaches to childrearing would need to include consideration for one child with a disabling condition. Rieger found that these families used humor for a variety of reasons, including as a strategy to respond to negative or aggressive behaviors from the children. Rieger described these families as "empowered." She meant by this that parents who have a strengths-perspective when dealing with all of their children are parents who can not only cope well with a disabling condition, but who can help the family remain cohesive and positive in their relationships. Humor was a very positive force in that regard for these families. These parents viewed humor as a way to teach their children, including diminishing negative behaviors, a problem-solving tool, and a means to keep family relationships stable.

In 1994, developmental psychologists Joan E. Grusec and Jacqueline J. Goodnow developed a model of effective parenting with several factors prominent in their theory. They summarized many years of research concerning parental discipline methods that help children internalize their parents' values. These researchers are proponents of the use of induction and warmth with parents' discipline techniques.

Grusec and Goodnow (1994) proposed that research about humor and parental discipline is needed, but that it has been mostly ignored in the discipline of psychology. Grusec, in a June 2007 personal communication, stated that psychologists have not studied parents' use of humor with their children well and that it is sorely needed. Perhaps, as positive psychology gains ground, more research that includes humor will be forthcoming. Work like that of Alicja Rieger holds promise for more research and supports previous work from Rod A. Martin, discussed previously as a psychologist who is expert in the study of adult humor and coping.

Humor and Child Coping

Martin also wrote a chapter about the benefits of humor in children's lives (Martin 1989). He describes children's use of humor as a way for them to cope with growing up. He states that the child who can face adversity with humor and laughter has a great skill in her coping repertoire. Conflict, frustration, family tensions, and peer pressures in the neighborhood or school environments can promote children to behave in ways that are unacceptable to adults. Although dependent on the children's development of cognitive and social skills, Martin states that the use of humor to defuse conflict or assist in problem-solving gives the child a chance to reflect upon the problem from a "different perspective." Here again, we see the importance of the use of irony or incongruity.

Recall that the definition of humor includes the presence of an enjoyable incongruity. Earlier in this chapter, I described the twelve-year-old soccer players' ability to note and understand the facts and the incongruity of their stereotyping comments about Turkish people. The understanding of this incongruity, their stereotypes compared to a variety of people from Turkey and the United States, helped them shift their views. This "different perspective" or frame of reference shift enabled the children to pause, to see something ridiculous that they were asserting and resolve their tension. In circumstances like this, children are able to note the humor and see how it can defuse conflict by reducing any threat to themselves or others they may perceive. Humor helps children cope with others.

Martin goes on to say that such children who possess a good sense of humor, this ability to shift their frame of reference, are viewed positively by their peers and adults and are believed to be healthier adults, psychologically. According to Martin, good use of humor helps people maintain their relational bonds. Overall, the psychologically healthy child can use humor appropriately. A good sense of humor is a signal to others that interactions with the child will be pleasant; the child's good Ph is evident to all.

The psychologist Paul A. McGee edited a volume about the development of children's humor (McGee 1989). He described the then early efforts of a handful of psychologists and educators to understand the development of humor in children and the possible practical applications of this skill to other development. McGee wrote that the development of humor is related to other skill-building, just as Masten and Martin discussed. These skills include cognitive and social skills, but just how humor translates to other skill-building is not yet fully understood. McGhee wrote that humor enhances children's development by encouraging learning and positive emotion, that likewise social bonds are strengthened. Teachers' sense of humor likely assists children's learning, but at that time, not much data existed to support this. Quantifying this might be difficult, but it's a good research question nonetheless. More recent study has generated data to support the use of humor in the classroom. Let's examine a few of these.

Humor and Teachers

Psychologist Helen Patrick and her colleagues looked at the first days of school for a group of twelve-year-old children (Patrick et al. 2003). They found that teachers who used humor were more likely to provide supportive environments in their classroom and had children who reported being more engaged with the curriculum at the year's end. These teachers' positive views and expectations for their students were communicated with doses of appropriate humor that helped these children succeed.

Public health scientists Katie Buston and Daniel Wight found from their studies in the United Kingdom that children participate more actively in classrooms when they have teachers with a strong sense of humor. These researchers found that the children asked more questions and engaged in less disruptive behavior when they had teachers who were humorous than the students whose teachers were more somber. Enthusiasm was another factor related to the children's success, but they summarized their findings by saying that, overall, the teachers with a strong sense of humor presided over successful classrooms (Buston and Wight 2004).

From Taiwan, data has emerged that show how a sense of humor in teachers is related to creative teaching. Jeou-Shyan Horng and her colleagues found that teachers who had creative ideas, a willingness to explore new teaching tools, and self-confidence about their teaching also displayed a keen sense of humor. These authors believe that successful, creative instruction relies upon many factors, but that a sense of humor is integral to this instruction (Horng et al. 2005). Other developmental correlates of children's play and use of humor are found in the literature as well.

Humor and Other Developmental Correlates

A study from Greece about the playfulness of preschool children and their motor activity development was examined by physical education experts Efthimios Trevlas and her colleages (Trevlas, Matsouka, and Zachopoulou 2003). Teachers' use of humor was not examined in this study. Rather, these Greek scientists asked teachers to report on the children's playfulness and overall development. They found that the children's physical, social, and cognitive spontaneity were related to their playfulness. The children who were high in playfulness were high in creative and critical thinking. They went on to say that children with these abilities have been shown to be psychologically healthy; that a sense of humor, curiosity, tolerance, and inventiveness are thought to be high in these children as well. These data reveal that preschool children use motor activity to learn about their worlds and those who can find a sense of joy in their movement have other skills developing simultaneously. What a marvelous support for the importance of children's developing use of fun!

A Columbian researcher of children's cognitive development, Rebeca Puche-Navarro, described her studies that have revealed a relationship between children's overall thinking ability and humor. Puche-Navarro found that children between two and four years of age have quite a shift in their "representational thinking." This simply means that by age four, children can often use a cognitive process that assists them in either producing a humorous event or understanding one. They can use one thing to represent another. One example will help explain this. A four-year-old child who does not usually like to eat vegetables notes that her mother is talking with her in a concerned way about her not eating vegetables. The child removes a banana from a bowl of fruit on the table, peels it, and says to her mother, "See, I'm eating a carrot, Mommy!" with a smile. This form of substitution or production of the incongruity is a form of representational thinking and tells researchers such as Puche-Navarro that humor development is an excellent way to examine how children think. By examining the development of humor in children, researchers can learn about other facets of their cognitive development. Puche-Navarro (2004) goes on to say that this area of study is very new in psychology, but a rich possibility for future study.

A summary list of positive psychological growth in children and its relationship to humor seems worthwhile here. Overall, children who are raised by parents and teachers with a dose of fun are also physically, socially, and cognitively engaged. Children who develop a good sense of humor, who can appreciate it and produce it, are thought to be children with good Ph. Researchers believe that children's sense of humor and playfulness is related to the following:

1 Positive emotion
2 Building and maintaining relationships
3 Academic success
4 Independence
5 Coping
6 Physical/motor skill
7 Representational thinking

Caring adults in children's lives contribute to this success by encouraging the use of humor in positive ways, thus showing children one means to establish good Ph that can remain with them throughout their lives.

Caveats and Practical Suggestions

Researchers such as Fry and Martin caution that the understanding of humor in adults' and children's lives from a psychological perspective is nascent, just now gaining attention. We have much work to do. When psychologists discuss "relationships" between variables, recall that this tells the reader that a line of causality cannot be established. These researchers remind us that the development of humor and its relationship to physical and psychological health is complex. We cannot say that humor *causes* people to be physically healthier, smarter, or happier than those without humor, at least not with data to support these claims. Rather, we must rely on what data we have and continue the research. The evocative, philosophical uses of humor can be discussed and evaluated at "face value," however. Who among us cannot say that our lives have been enriched because of others' use of humor or a well-developed sense of humor in ourselves? Not many of us, probably. We have looked at the data concerning humor in adults and children's lives and its relationship to physical and psychological health. Yet we only have scant data about the ways caring adults transmit humor and fun to children.

Earlier in this chapter we examined the position of psychologists Joan Grusec and Jacqueline Goodnow about humor and parenting. They lamented the lack of data about humor and its place in their model. As is so often the case in researching the complexities of human behavior, we need more research. The science in this chapter is sound, yet remembering the nature of correlational research brings the reader back to the question of how fun-raising is related to good Ph in children.

While psychology as a science has only a small amount of data to support the uses of humor in children's lives, most adults can likely agree that such fun-promotion is worthwhile. Fun-raising can bring everyone joy and help people maintain their relationships. Children's cognitive, social, and physical development are related to fun-raising. Adults' use of induction, warmth, and humor can be growth promoting for everyone in a family. Recall that in chapter 4 we discussed how a play time that includes a little mess, an out of the ordinary play activity such as mud pies or finger-painting, can be fun for children and adults. Such activities provide new avenues of discovery for children.

In thinking about the importance of fun-raising for children, we have considered many possible vignettes that can bring families joy. Below, I also write about a family vacation. Fun-raising should provide fun for everyone in a family, but even this can be quite a tall order for parents. When people are outside of their normal routines, they may be open not only to new avenues of discovery, but also to stressors not considered previously. Parents who can approach a novel event with good humor and fun-raising in mind can make any day an enjoyable one, with opportunities for learning and a belly laugh possible for all concerned. Here are a few tips for facilitating a family's time away together that can mean a positive, enjoyable experience.

The Family Vacation: Fun-Raising at Its Best

When adults in a family wish to bring joy and a little fun into their lives and their children's, they often try to arrange a short break from the usual routine, a getaway from the mundane. But just consider how many comic movies have been made about family vacations that prove disastrous. Hollywood has seen parents' pain and put its own brand of humor on interpretations of the family vacation. Traveling with children can be tough, but the rewards of a well-planned, kid-friendly vacation can be great for adults and children. Besides mileage and cost, there are other factors that can be weighed to help adults with their vacation planning. The following eight rules can help insure that all family members participate in some fun-raising.

1   Discuss the planning of an activity with each family member that is age-appropriate. This signals to children that they belong to the family and their opinions are valued. Very young children may only be able to help decide which park to go to on a given day on the trip, but children around ages seven or eight and older can be good assistants with the planning. Such an inclusion of opinions not only promotes that sense of belongingness discussed in chapter 4, but also helps assure the children will enjoy their time away. Planning time together sends the message to children that negotiation and compromise are valued and is a good model for other issues that may arise in children's lives concerning groups of people.

2   Remember each child's age when planning activities and rest periods. If a family has more than one child, each age must be factored into the vacation choices. If a family has more than one parent, family members can be divided up along age and interest during the vacation,

but time spent together is important also. If parents divide up activities, be sure to take turns being with different children. Part of why families go trekking is to reconnect with each other without the interference of the daily grind. Moms, do not miss the chance to watch a ball game that you normally would not choose. Dads, how about an art museum? If the adults are not gender-challenged, wonderful! Just trade-off to get out of your usual comfort zone. If you can all go together to each attraction, great. If anyone needs a break from one family member, manage that as well.

3   Find something fun for everyone each day. For children, this can be as small as a restaurant with wait-staff in animal costumes. Children need child-friendly activities to help them maintain a positive mood. Activities that include movement are sure to please preschool and early elementary-aged children. Pre-adolescents, adolescents, and adults can always use physical activity as well.

4   If the adults find they are becoming stressed, note it. Parents can model good humor and optimism as a means to defuse conflict or difficulty. Say out loud, "We're on vacation. We can handle this." A lost bag or an entire carload of lost people can be overcome with a little good cheer. Adults who cope are helping children learn a very valuable skill.

5   If the adults or children are becoming homesick, perhaps it *is* time to go home. If airline tickets or other non-negotiable factors are a part of this decision-making, adults can find ways to make the mood brighter. Return to the restaurant with animal-costumed waiters. Find a new vista or beauty to enjoy. Encourage children to talk about the parts of the vacation they have enjoyed. Allow them to make a phone call to a friend or a relative. Part of the fun of travel is the fresh perspective and appreciation gained of home.

6   Vacations do not have to be budget-splitting or time intensive. A "camp-out" in the back yard, one new vista a few miles from home, or one night away that means quality time together can be enjoyable. Fun-raising can be small or large.

7   Adults' ability to use humor and laughter as a means to stay connected through good days and those days that do not turn out so well is a wonderful model for children to emulate. Children appreciate all forms of fun, positive emotion, and good will. Adults who are cognizant of this can promote fun-raising and good Ph at the same time.

8   Have fun!

Summary and Musing

At the beginning of the film *An Inconvenient Truth*, Al Gore introduced himself thus: "I used to be the next president of the United States!" He began with this ironic statement to help his audience feel at ease. What a great way to begin the very serious topic of global warming. Gore does not bring up his past again in the movie except to discuss his boyhood home as a rural paradise that is environmentally vulnerable today. It appears that Gore has found a new way to make his contribution to society and he lets the audience know quickly that it is the future he is concerned about. The fact that he uses a bit of humor to introduce himself is a signal to the audience that he has had a crisis and yet is ready to go forward, much like Keltner and Bonanno (1997) describe in their study of the bereaved.

Psychologists are beginning to assemble a better stock of data about the benefits of humor to adult health. There is some much needed discussion about fun-raising in different forms in psychology, and the literature base for resounding support of the importance of humor and laughter in children's lives remains small. My not-so-amusing musing is that psychologists must be a somber lot who could use some fun-raising of their own!

Within psychology, you will find rigorous, relevant research about warmth and nurturance in parenting. From the adult literature base, more is known today than twenty years ago about laughter and MRIs, physical health's relationship to humor, etc. Yet the same cannot be said of humor's place in adults' responsibility to children. It appears that for many psychologists there exists a reverence for adults' responsibility to children but without much attention to fun-raising. Let's change this.

Many philosophers have written that people should focus on enjoying life and live every day to the fullest. This full-fledged, full-bodied living should include humor, laughter, and fun. Fun-raising for children has merits in many respects. The correlates of humor and laughter are positive additions to people's relationships and to other development as well. When famous psychologists such as Joan E. Grusec and Jacqueline J. Goodnow state that the links between humor and parenting need to be researched better, we should pay attention. Psychologists who are expert in humor's stress-buffering effects such as Rod A. Martin and Herbert M. Lefcourt state that these data are known in adults, but we can only extrapolate the findings to children.

These are reminders that we have much work to do. Data that support the need for fun-raising may be meager today, but enough exists to encourage adults to promote fun-raising with children and their healthy Ph. Fun-raising is the sixth measure for good Ph. Adults in children's lives can bring joy to them, model humor's benefits, and scaffold this development in children. Clearly, fun-raising can be a very important part of children's lives and the adults in children's lives can be enriched as well. Overall development, social relationships, and fun are interrelated and require psychologists to research them further. Adults' use of fun in their relationships with children promotes positive outcomes and good Ph.

These solid foundations in important relationships that show sensitivity to others more broadly are the topic of the next chapter.

Chapter 8

Tolerance and Social Activism

Teachers are moving about the cafeteria with the peer-elected student leaders in tow, urging the other children to try a new table, away from their usual group of friends. The day is "Mix-It-Up-At-Lunch Day," an event designed to bring children into new encounters with their peers. This event provides the more outgoing children with the opportunity to say hello to children who may benefit from a chance to feel less isolated, more connected to their peers. While one hello is a pretty short greeting, the event is also designed to encourage children to eat their lunches with those who they do not know. The goal is for children from different social groups to eat together as peers – to get to know each other so that new relationships can be built or, at the least, new understanding of the "other" may occur. The school leaders have been prepared to function as a model for the other children to emulate. At the end of the lunch period, only the school leaders designated by the school faculty have moved from their usual tables and are seen visiting graciously with children they have not met before. It's a start!

The seventh measure for good Ph is the development of tolerance for others who children see as different from themselves and the awareness that everyone deserves an equal opportunity at life's joys, including work and school. This is the essence of "social justice." This phrase is found in the codes of ethics of the helping professions such as psychology and social work, which ask of their members a commitment to action that is known as "social activism." Actions are needed that promote the welfare of all in societies where hierarchies and inequalities abound. "Prosocial behaviors" – those that are positive for all concerned – can be taught and develop in children under the warm tutelage of caring adults. As the 21st century unfolds, it appears we need these positive connections as much or more so than we did in the last century.

Adults who care about children can encourage and teach prosocial behavior, tolerance, and social activism such that children can practice days such as "Mix-It-Up-At-Lunch" with grace and an openness and commitment to others. Lessons about tolerance that help guide people's beliefs and actions, and activism that enriches people personally, as well as whole communities, must begin early. Children who are open to others and who are committed to goals outside of themselves are healthier people psychologically, and they help make the world a better place for everyone. Just how these very large goals are met to promote good Ph in children and others is the subject of this chapter. Large goals they are, but they're possible with the help of caring adults.

Research in psychology about the promotion of tolerance and social activism in children is scarce. We will examine some studies that date back to the earliest writings about prosocial behavior and some more recent, specific data about promoting tolerance and activism in children today. I will rely upon much of the work already delineated in this book to draw the reader a map by means of which adults can guide children. I will also rely upon my own theoretical orientation of ecological systems and social cognitive theory to provide links between what is known and the promotion of good Ph in children who espouse tolerance and act on others' behalf.

Let's begin by examining the cafeteria example described above. In previous chapters I used happy, positive examples to set the stage for measures that promote the healthy psychological development of children. The example above is less positive in that the difficulty the children have with building relationships across borders is evident. Meeting new people or conversing with those less known to the children must have seemed like an insurmountable task to them. They were still, uncomfortable, unwilling to heed the pleas of their teachers and their school leaders. What events and development had transpired previously that made the children so silent, so noncompliant? Some research in psychology exists that helps us understand the children's reluctance to mix it up at lunch.

First, this special day is one in a school year of more than 200 days. It is possible that the children have not had much practice at this, or many chances to observe adults model this behavior. Adults rarely provide these structured opportunities for children. People often group themselves into categories by means of such things as physical features or interests. Selfless motivations to meet new people, to treat those you do not know with interest and kindness, is a very tall order for adults, let alone children.

Much of this book has been about adults examining their behavior so that they may be better able to promote positive growth in children. This chapter is no different. Adults who encourage children to act in prosocial ways, in settings such as school cafeterias, whole communities, or even globally, often need to develop this skill as well. How many adults can say that they try to meet a new person who looks "different" to them regularly or even once a year? Difference in the form of physical or cognitive ability, skin color, facial features, social class, sexual orientation, or even interest can mean reluctance on the part of adults to engage each other socially. Many adults do not seek out experiences that would help them learn about others. Caring adults who serve as models for openness and social interactions with different others are needed.

Designating a few children as leaders means that only those with that special responsibility will act. Look at this study from Geoffrey Maruyama (Maruyama, Fraser, and Miller 1982). It remains one of the best examples of the need for designating responsibility in order for children to act in prosocial ways. These social psychologists set the stage for their experiment in the front room of a home on Halloween night. The researchers asked groups of trick-or-treating children to donate their candy to children who were in the hospital. When the researchers said to one child, "You are the leader" this child donated candy to the hospital jar and a few children followed that lead. However, when the researchers said to each child pointedly, "We are relying on you, and you, and you, and you," almost every child donated some of their candy. When no child was assigned responsibility for donating, only a few gave some of their candy. The designation of personal responsibility was made clear to the children and they responded in prosocial ways.

In looking at the cafeteria example, it is evident that adults have a very large role in promoting tolerance and social justice. Providing children with models for behavior, chances for practice, and the teaching of personal responsibility to act positively promotes positive behaviors in children. Recall that chapter 7 began with two children eating their dinners after working much of the day at the women's shelter. Adults who cared about their development were there also, working themselves, supervising the children, and making their values of service to the community explicit to the children. The children's view of their time spent was that it was more like fun-raising than fund-raising. Joy in their service was evident. Caring adults gave these children personal responsibility, modeled the behavior themselves in a community setting, and explicitly provided the opportunity for the children's action. The outcome was positive for all concerned.

Children's commitment to others and the building of whole communities is possible when adults:

1 use induction, explain the need for tolerance and activism and their rewards;
2 are open to and welcoming of children's questions about difference;
3 give children responsibility to form connections with others;
4 provide opportunities for social activism;
5 provide models of positive behaviors with others;
6 make their values of tolerance and social justice explicit.

Values can not only inoculate children against negative influences, but they also serve to promote positive behaviors in children. Children's important "others," such as parents, teachers, and community and religious leaders, can promote these beliefs and actions. The role of parents in the teaching of tolerance and activism is examined first.

Parental Word and Deed

Two early studies stand out in the literature about how parents' beliefs and actions can promote the welfare of others. Perry London (1970) studied Christians who helped Jewish people escape the Nazis during World War II. David Rosenhan (1970) studied white civil rights workers in the United States when civil rights activism was just gaining ground in the late 1950s and early 1960s. These researchers wanted to know what motivated the people who risked their lives for "social others," those whose categories of origin and place in society differed from their own. Perry London found three motivating themes in the people he studied. These Christians had a sense of adventure, a sense of being on the margins of their society, and one strong, moral parent who taught and behaved in activist ways to promote the welfare of others. London wrote: "What was expressed directly most often was the admiration for a parent or adherence to [the parents'] ... strong moralistic opinions" (London 1970: 249).

David Rosenhan found similar results in his study participants from the early Civil Rights Movement. These are the stirring words of Rosenhan as he described the activists' methods and goals:

> The civil rights workers followed closely the Ghandian model and nonviolence was their cardinal principle ... central concerns were equal rights and integration. Equality of education was [central] but not far behind were voting rights, poverty, rights to employment and rights to freedom of transport. The battlefield was still almost entirely in the South. It was then difficult to anticipate that it would spread to the North, to its cities and its slums, and to the universities. (Rosenhan 1970: 256)

Rosenhan's findings were similar to London's. The activists who spent the longest time and most effort to support the Civil Rights Movement had positive relationships with parents and came from families who were psychologically healthy. Further, these young adults who reported their warm relationships and healthy family backgrounds also reported at least one parent who was an activist as well. As Rosenhan stated, these parents who "were themselves fully committed to an altruistic cause during some extended period of the respondents' formative years" (p. 262) promoted social activism. Rosenhan described those parents who not only taught prosocial or altruistic behavior, but who *lived* their values as well. The young adults had parental models of prosocial behavior as well as verbal messages about concern for others and the importance of acting upon one's beliefs. These parents made their values explicit to their children.

Recall that in previous chapters I outlined the importance of teaching with induction and warmth, as well as the importance of modeling the positive behaviors we wish the children in our care to exhibit. Albert Bandura's (2001) social cognitive theory provides adults with a good framework for raising children who are personally responsible for their own actions and the welfare of others. Children must be taught the lessons of prosocial behavior, tolerance, and social action so that they have an opportunity to consider them, and they must see important adults in their world engaging in these acts of selfless struggle so that models are evident. Children need opportunities to practice these lessons so that they can understand them as important for everyone's positive development. Children need these messages throughout their childhoods so that their commitment to social activism is present by the time they are adolescents.

Other Parental Influences

When children are first learning about their environments at home, empathy emerges from them in concert with empathic verbalizations and behaviors from their parents. Caring and concern about others begin with parents. As children grow and encounter social others in different contexts, these same empathic responses are related to the children's prosocial behavior toward others. In a study conducted by psychologists Janet Strayer and William Roberts (2004), parents were asked about their empathy toward their children and the children, aged five to thirteen years, were asked about how they were parented. The children who reported they had emotionally healthy parents demonstrated empathy toward others and prosocial behavior as well. "Emotionally healthy" meant that the parents had formed empathic bonds with their children, who modeled their prosocial behavior toward others. This study supports the need for early empathic parenting skills that will be related to children's behavior as they develop. A few demographic variables related to parents have been found to be related to broader prosocial behavior in children, as evidenced in the following studies.

Constance Flanagan is a psychologist expert in the promotion of civic engagement in children. Flanagan and her colleague, C. J. Tucker, published a study in 1999 in which they found that the higher a mother's education and the household income of a school district, the more likely adolescents saw societal responsibility to ameliorate poverty and homelessness in the United States. These same adolescents reported that they were from families who focused on compassion for others and they believed that more prosocial life goals were needed across society. Many young people see their societal responsibilities. Recall that in chapter 6 we examined a publication called *The American Freshman* produced by the Higher Education Research Institute (2005) and found that the entering college freshmen class of 2005 valued working in their communities for the betterment of others at a higher rate than the previous entering freshmen class. These freshmen saw a societal need they were willing to respond to in prosocial ways. Their social activism was evident.

These data give hope that prosocial values, beliefs, and actions of important adults in children's lives are gaining ground in the United States. What can we make of Flanagan and Tucker's findings? Perhaps more education helps us examine our beliefs and others' as well, and more income means a chance to consider the privileges of some and not others. In fact, psychologists who actively promote peace assert that values of tolerance and human rights are supported when people are educated about diverse cultures and lifestyles in the world (see Pyszczynski, Greenberg, and Solomon 2003).

Where else might parents find support for their activism that they wish to model for their children? Often, religious teachings are a resource for adults. Look at these words of John Wesley, one of the founders of the Methodist Church:

> Do all the good you can, by all the means you can, in all the ways you can, in all the places you can, at all the times you can, to all the people you can, as long as ever you can. (Wesley 1915: 423)

Wesley's words are echoed today in many families.

A psychologist expert in the relationships of African-American youth, Judith Smetana studied adolescents' civic involvement and found that mothers' early teaching and action around religious activities influenced adolescents' own spirituality (see Smetana and Metzger 2005). This spirituality was also related to the adolescents' reports of later civic involvement. Those adolescents from a spiritually rich family would more likely engage in helping the larger community themselves. All of the world's great religions encourage their followers to engage in connecting with others, helping those less fortunate and promoting peace. Education and religion are two pathways to social activism.

To summarize these data, it appears that the cultural prescription in the United States that stresses individual success and autonomy may be changing. Perhaps more adults are communicating today than in the 20th century the need for children to develop personal responsibility toward others. We can hope that messages about connecting with others, including those whose life circumstances are very difficult and the need for advocacy and action by more fortunate others, are increasing. Perhaps the collectivist spirit that psychologist Harry Triandis (1994) writes so eloquently about has now taken root in the United States. This global view begins with children who understand that their connections to others bring more understanding and social justice to the world.

Teachers and Tolerance

As in previous chapters, I wish to encourage all adults who are responsible for their children to engage in the facilitation of children's psychological health. Good Ph for children is dependent on all the adults in children's lives. Teachers are a very important part of this promotion of tolerance and social activism.

Recall that in chapter 4 we discussed the importance of the family as an environment of belonging. Relationships in which trust and respect are paramount help promote future relationships. Similarly, teachers who promote social responsibility in their classrooms are considered those teachers who are also promoting prosocial behavior. A sense of belonging to a larger social group brings with it notions of individual responsibility and a willingness to consider others' wellbeing, along with personal wellbeing. The school environment provides another opportunity for belonging and reaching out to others.

By the late adolescent period, or age fourteen to fifteen, children's feelings about belonging to their school peer groups may override their sense of belonging at home. At the very least, we have some data that show how feelings of belonging at school, a sense of school-as-community, are related to children's good Ph. Psychologist Heather M. Chipuer reported in her 2001 study that children's sense of belonging to their schools was instrumental in helping them avoid loneliness and being more open to others. Chipuer wrote that the children's social selves were psychologically healthy if they experienced a connection to their school communities and that this connection would pave the way for broader prosocial behavior to come. Teachers were instrumental in this regard. How can schools capitalize on this finding in order to promote more positive feelings and social activism in general?

Many schools across the United States have begun requiring "service learning" projects of their students in high school. Service learning combines curriculum and community service components to promote students' understanding of material. For example, high school students who wish to become teachers may study child development in the classroom and be required to volunteer at an elementary school during the week. Required service learning for students is relatively new in the United States, but we already have some data that show it is a very positive addition to schools' curriculum. Such outcomes as positive contributions to the community, the students' psychological health, and even the enhancement of learning the specific curriculum in which the service component is embedded have been found. (Psychologist Amy Strage's 2004 article is a good summary of these findings.)

By the year 2000, approximately one-third of U.S. schools had service learning components (Billig 2000). The prosocial benefits reaped by these youngsters included more selfless views, increases in tolerance and commitment to multiculturalism, and an ethos that included service to others as an important goal. The task of integrating service learning into all schools looks formidable, but it is much needed, given these outcomes for children's good Ph and society in general.

Reed A. Larson, a psychologist who is a renowned expert in adolescent development, wrote in 2000 that educators need to find ways to enhance students' intrinsic motivation that includes concentration over an extended period of time. He believes that children's "positive development" can be enhanced with a focus on intrinsic motivation. Larson laments that much of the high school curriculum is not designed with this in mind and that the challenge for educators and parents alike is to allow adolescents more freedom of choice in their learning. When solely adults structure adolescents' learning, adolescents are "other" motivated, often performing for rewards that adults have set forth without an intrinsic commitment to mastery. Larson states of the responses he gathered from his research with adolescents about their school day, "they read like a script from Bart Simpson" (Larson 2000: 170). The adolescents reported boredom and a lack of engagement in their school work, as though they were waiting for someone to show them the joys of learning.

Larson goes on to state that John Dewey was correct when he wrote in 1938 that adults must "allow" children to use their new-found learning, that skill mastery and true engagement can only be gained by *doing*. Larson asserts that structured voluntary activities are one route to facilitating high intrinsic motivation with concentration over a period of time. Similar to the concept of service learning, this extracurricular volunteering, including community and religious service activities, may provide such environments to promote intrinsic motivation for tolerance and social activism. Larson believes that adults interested in children's overall development should facilitate more volunteer activities that bring them joy and intrinsic motivation.

Larger Social Environments

In chapter 3 we discussed the importance of extracurricular activities as a socializing agent for children. Reed Larson states that the nature of these groups means that children's intrinsic motivation is supported because much of the daily running of these groups is structured by the children themselves. Whether they are on debate teams or organizing religious activities to serve their communities, they are engaged in charting much of their own course with adults who assist this development. Adult scaffolding is provided and the learning is collaborative. Such outcomes as better grade point averages as older adolescents, and more volunteerism at later ages, have been associated with children who are actively engaged in their larger communities as high school students. These data provide a glimpse of the importance of allowing children a sense of agency as adults try to facilitate and scaffold prosocial activities that children may engage in. Larson says that understanding the importance of children's intrinsic motivation to behave competently can be a part of their overall positive development.

We return to the work of Constance Flanagan. In her chapter in the *Handbook of Adolescent Psychology* (2004), she writes that the reciprocal nature of adults who volunteer their time in extracurricular activities with children and the subsequent civic engagement of the children's time is a "virtuous circle." Those adults who are teaching prosocial engagement are promoting it with children who trust them. Concurrently, these children have more positive views of others in general when compared to uninvolved peers. Collective goals that are structured by children for their groups with the help of caring adults mean that children's development is enhanced. The children are learning how to structure and meet goals for a social good. Their own good Ph is promoted and the community and larger society benefit from their work.

Flanagan's discussion takes us back to the importance of parents. She states that adolescents who are actively engaged in their communities have parents who are engaged there as well. Although social class is one factor that predicts civic engagement – higher parental income is related to more civic involvement – activism in communities is found across class when religious affiliations are considered. That is, less economically advantaged families often do engage in social activism in relation to their religious institutions' community work. When provided opportunities, all children can develop civic engagement. Smetana and Metzger's (2005) work supports these data.

Tolerance and a commitment to social activism are promoted when children are able to help others in need or when they seize opportunities to learn about social others who they have not encountered before. Such action also means opportunities for discussion with caring adults about the meaning of social activism. Adults must be available when children begin to question themselves and their society. The adolescent in chapter 6 who bought the t-shirt that depicted Native American chiefs with a caption that read "Fighting Terrorism Since 1492" was given a chance to display his dislike for the treatment of the Native people by the U.S. government. The discussion between the father and the child was necessary to assist the child's examination of his own values and resolve surrounding this social justice issue. The father made explicit his approval of the child's questioning and allowed the child to act upon his own beliefs. Adults who wish to promote tolerance and social justice among children must learn to deal with their own biases and social justice actions as well. This is the topic of the next section.

Teaching Tolerance and Social Activism

When caring adults attempt to teach children their values, including tolerance for others and how to act upon their beliefs, they can find it a struggle. Adults in children's lives often need some assistance in confronting their own place in society and their own biases – biases that can make teaching tolerance more difficult. The work of two advocates of the importance of teaching teachers to work within a social justice framework is a good place to begin. In 1992, Gerald Weinstein and Kathy Obear offered teachers strategies to become more competent at teaching social justice concepts. These college educators asked teachers to consider how their own development contributed to their teaching of tolerance. The following is a summary of their strategies.

Teachers should
1   Have an awareness of their own social identities, including but not limited to ethnic origin, gender, religion, class, ableism, etc.
2   Confront their biases. Ask how their circumstances are informed by such concepts as "white privilege," "gender privilege," etc.
3   Examine how they respond to bias spoken by dominant members of a group about targeted groups. For example, explore what should be said of children's use of "retarded," "gay," or "lame" as adjectives that demean others.
4   Remember that all adults are still learning how to confront their biases and respond to others.
5   Recall that students' (children's) approval is very important, but must be weighed with the importance of social justice issues. Confronting with warmth is possible.
6   Learn to deal with the emotional intensity sometimes displayed by children surrounding these issues, as well as their own. When adults fear losing control of a classroom or fear losing a warm connection with their children, tentative responses may occur. Be aware when this happens and deal with it as well. Take a break; dive back in.

Let's examine what Weinstein and Obear (1992) ask teachers to do. These tips can also work well with parents or any other adults who have children in their care. First, adults must examine what social categories have helped or deterred their own positive development. Adults should consider their family backgrounds, ethnic origins, religious beliefs, physical ability or "ableness," and other categories that are integral to who they are. For example, as a teacher, I often have

Euro-American students who say they have no ethnic origin when I ask them to engage in this discussion in class. These white students who attend college in the United States believe by virtue of their majority positions, both in number and in power, that their ethnic group is pervasive and in no need of delineation or examination. They are experiencing "white privilege." I ask such students to confront this bias by gently but directly saying to them, "I think you are speaking from a place of white privilege." Students who are unfamiliar with this phrase – and there are many – work with me in order to sort through this bias, previously unknown to them. Confronting our own biases serves to make adults more open to questioning by children when we wish to teach tolerance. The good Ph of adults helps promote the same in children.

How adults respond to spoken biases or actions is important for children's learning. Recall the "soccer dad" who stopped the stereotyping of Turkish people by the children in his car. He went on to gently encourage them to consider their positions and brought some mirth to the lesson through his own comfortableness with the situation. The father showed the children in his care that he did indeed care about them as he challenged their stereotyped views of others. This is an example of a very successful confrontation. However, not all of us are so skilled with every possible confrontation. Adults must remember that they are learning about tolerance and social activism every day, just like the children. It is difficult for adults to risk the good will of the children in their care to stop a discussion and engage them in a confrontation about bias. However, whether it be students in a classroom or a soccer team in a car, adults are responsible to help shape children's and students' ideas about social others and bring more tolerance to the world.

Finally, it is often the case that tolerance and social justice issues carry with them a high degree of emotional intensity. When people feel slighted or defensive about their positions, their cognitive capabilities may seem to disengage and their emotional selves take over. Most people have difficulty thinking well when they believe they are being attacked. Children need adults to assist them with hearing the confrontation as caring, words spoken or actions done for their benefit. Adults are not so different. The maturity that comes with age is no guarantee of a thoughtful, well-formed response to intolerance or lack of social justice. All of us can have difficulty with the emotional content often inherent in others' invitations to change. When adults find that their classrooms or homes are fraught with tension about intolerance, adults can ask everyone to take a breath, take a break, and consider quietly what intolerance has transpired. Perhaps we can ask children to write or draw about their experience as a way to get them back into a clearer cognitive mode with less emotional content. Adults may need to do the same. Not that emotional content is without value – far from it! It is just that reasoning through others' positions about tolerance may require much thought and focus.

As adults, we ask ourselves which battles to choose with the children in our care. The very issues that make adults nervous are often those that children are nervous about as well. The father driving the soccer team heard the children speaking negatively about people from Turkey and he chose to stop such stereotyping by naming the action and asking them to "Tell me a little more about that." He knew he needed a few seconds to calm himself down. This invitation also gave the father more information about what motivated this negative talk, as well as time to form his words of caution and tolerance that he knew must be delivered to the children with warmth. The father used humor to help him make his point and the children were able to integrate his teaching with their previous views. Tolerance and social justice were promoted by the father's social activism, his commitment to speaking when he heard a demeaning interaction.

Child Development, Good Ph, Tolerance, and Social Justice

In this book we have examined the various roles that adults have in children's lives. The various contexts of home, school, and communities are places where children's development occurs. Within these teaching environments children's cognitive, social, and larger political selves are shown to be important for children's good Ph. The children's good Ph gives us hope for building better societies for all in the future. As Constance Flanagan (2004) writes, each generation of children will have different historical events and patterns to deal with. Their development of civic responsibility and activism will necessarily change from one generation to the next because of these differing challenges.

As Urie Bronfenbrenner's (1986) ecological systems theory posits, each generation must deal with the historical context in which they are reared. Children's development relies on interactions with adults and other children that promote their good Ph. The complications of the world impinge on this development and tolerance-seeking adults are needed today more than ever. The 21st century is fraught with strife and a decided lack of tolerance is seen among the people who are at war across the globe. It behooves the adults in a free society and, arguably around the world in less free societies, to work to promote children's development along all of these important domains.

Cognitive and social development occur when children are actively engaged in their worlds with the help of caring adults. Their good Ph is dependent upon adults who seek tolerance and justice for all. Global tolerance and social justice are dependent upon the next generation. Let's not leave this burden for our children without such tools as their "value shields and beacons," as discussed in chapter 6. Social activism is its reward for our children.

Early connections with parents and other caring adults set children on a course of relationship development that will serve them well throughout their lives. Social commitments and compassion for people and the environment that need human intervention or repair are promoted by adults concerned about the early development of children. These early bonds, including those with other children, are the building blocks of good Ph that help children look outside of themselves to engage in civic responsibility and service to others. When the important adults in children's lives take their responsibility for rearing the next generation seriously and with informed ways of knowing such as those which psychological research can provide, we become better able to assist all children to be the activists of the future. The practical applications of the psychological research discussed in this book provide many opportunities for adults to help children build their good Ph.

As you embark upon finding more knowledge to assist your growth and that of the children in your care, take time to find other resources that will make you a better parent and a better teacher. The appendix at the end of this book is structured to help you with more learning. Much of the reading list for the development of tolerance in children and adults comes from a social psychologist who is known for her work in promoting tolerance: Dr. Kim Case. Case designed and researched discussion groups that were called "White Women Against Racism" for many years and that serve as a model for how people with privilege can examine their own biases and work for social justice. Case and her spouse Kent Case also have a wonderful library of children's books about promoting tolerance (see the appendix).

As individuals, we can make a difference for ourselves and in our children's lives. Look at these stirring words from Margaret Mead: "Never doubt that a small group of people can bring about change. Indeed, it is the only method that has ever worked." I interviewed a civil rights worker for the preparation of this book and three notes from him stood out for me. A renowned historian, Dr. Bruce Palmer (personal communication, March 1, 2007) said this of his experience in the 1960s in the United States. He began as a civil rights worker because he was in a relationship that mattered to him and his partner was active in the movement. His parents had a social conscience and when he proposed to them that he would join the movement, his mother supported him fully and told him she envied him. Finally, he reminded me that the Civil Rights Movement was initiated with very few people. Their talents were evident to Palmer, but their numbers were small. The United States changed because of a small group of talented people who were social activists. Adults have influence in children's lives and their current societies need all generations of people to work for tolerance and social justice. These begin with our earliest relationships.

In this book, I have emphasized relationships as the way to build children's futures. Their good Ph can be promoted with the seven measures we have discussed. Adults who promote children's development with caring and warmth function across skill domains. That is, parents, teachers, and other important adults help promote children's overall growth. Adults who stimulate the cognitive, social, and physical development of children with their good Ph as the goal are promoting growth in everyone.

These goals are attainable. Build relationships in family and school environments that promote feelings of belonging and trust in others. Help children develop lasting friendships that will serve them throughout their lives. Teach the children your values and live them. Monitor the other influences in their lives. Have fun! Examine your own psychological health as well as biases. Help children to see their place in the world as change agents for the good of all. Tolerance and social justice have early beginnings in our children.

To use Constance Flanagan's phrase, the "virtuous circle" occurs when adults raise psychologically healthy children and they, in turn give back to their communities. The virtuous circle begins and ends with caring adults who are prepared for this important task. The children of the 21st century need us. Raising them with good Ph is possible and the rewards will be manifest for their good and that of others. Their good Ph will help them lead happy, successful lives. In turn, they will serve the world.

Appendix

Tolerance and Social Justice Resources

◆ ◆ ◆

General Resources

There are many great resources for adults to use with children.

1 I recommend becoming a member of an activist organization that promotes tolerance and social justice. One great organization of this kind is the Southern Poverty Law Center (SPLC). You can access this organization online at www.splcenter.org. This non-profit educational and legal foundation functions as a clearing house and activist leader for social good in the United States. This is the group that designed "Mix-It-Up-At-Lunch Day." They publish a magazine that members receive titled *Teaching Tolerance*. Every issue is full of sound tips for promoting tolerance and social activism in children. I learn something new about my fellow travelers on this Earth from every issue. The SPLC also makes free curriculum kits available to teachers. One example is "Responding to Hate at School: A Guide for Teachers, Counselors and Administrators."

2 When children are seeking activities to engage in, assist them in finding one that includes social activism. Many opportunities for service exist in all of our communities. One example is the Girl Scouts/Boy Scouts organization. Service to others is a hallmark of the work they ask of children. If you encounter a troop that is intolerant of some groups of children, seek another troop. Often, the Scout leaders' views prevail and we are all on the journey of overcoming bias at different levels. One recent book published about Eagle Scouts was written to detail some of the service engaged in by those who have attained this level of Scouting. They

have gone on to achieve national office, become members of the astronaut corps, save natural habitats, lead colleges, and serve as camp counselors as adults. Alvin Townley's *Legacy of Honor: The Values and Influence of America's Eagle Scouts* was published in 2007 by Thomas Dunne Books.

3 Youth Communication is a nonprofit youth development program that sells resource books for adults and adolescents, written by adolescents. Examples of some of their available titles are "Helping Others," "Growing up Black, Asian, Latino" (three titles), "Resilience," and "Mental Health." Find them at www.youthcomm. org or at 212–279–0708.

4 The Anti-Defamation League (ADL), in conjunction with Barnes and Noble publish a list of books that address social justice. The pamphlet they produce is called "Close the Book on Hate" and can be downloaded at the ADL's website: www.adl.org/prejudice/ default/asp. This list contains books for children and adults.

Books for Children

The children's book collection of Kim and Kent Case includes the following titles:

1 *King and King*. Linda de Haan and Stern Nijland. Two males become a couple.
2 *King and King and Family*. Linda de Hann and Stern Nijland. A male couple adopts a child.
3 *And Tango Makes Three*. Justin Richardson and Peter Parnell. The true story of two male penguins at the Central Park Zoo who become a couple and raise a baby penguin together.
4 *Heather Has Two Mommies*. Leslea Newman.
5 *Molly's Family*. Nancy Garden. A kindergarten child with two moms who attend Parents' Night together.
6 *We Adopted You, Benjamin Koo*. Linda Walvoord Girard. First person account of a child from Korea adopted in the United States.
7 *New Moon* is a magazine for girls about embracing girlhood and promotes tolerance and activism.
8 *William's Doll*. Charlotte Zolotow. William's grandmother buys him a doll so that he will learn nurturing skills.

9 *The Sissy Duckling*. Harvey Fierstein. Elmer the duck enjoys traditionally feminine activities and perseveres when his friends deride him.

10 *My Name was Hussein*. Hristo Kyuchukov. Ethnic violence means that children must adopt new beliefs or even change their names to survive.

11 *What if the Zebras Lost Their Stripes?* John Reitano. Black, white, or striped, we are all in the animal kingdom together.

12 *Zack's Story: Growing Up with Same Sex Parents*. Keith Greenberg. A first person account of Zack, who has two moms.

13 *Happy to Be Nappy*. bell hooks (author bell hooks does not capitalize her name). Be proud of who you are.

14 *Let's Talk About Race*. Julius Lester. Inside we are all the same.

15 *Black is Brown is Tan*. Arnold Adoff. A multi-ethnic family has many beautiful skin-tones.

16 *Spotty*. Margaret Rey. A spotted bunny leaves his all white bunny family only to find a spotted bunny family who is skeptical of a white bunny in their midst.

17 *Tusk Tusk*. David McKee. White and black elephants fight to their deaths while the peace loving ones escape. Generations later the surviving elephants emerge and are all gray.

18 *White Socks Only*. Evelyn Coleman. A young African-American girl drinks from an "All White" fountain and brings others to social activism as well.

19 *Why Should I Recycle?* Jen Green. Mr. Jones, a teacher, shows his students the benefit of recycling.

20 *ABC A Family Alphabet Book*. Bobbie Combs. Families are diverse.

Books for Adults

This booklist was generated in part by the members of Kim Case's groups titled "White Women Against Racism."

Children/education

Critical Multiculturalism: Rethinking Multicultural and Antiracist Education – Stephen May

Diversity in the Classroom, 2nd edition – Frances F. Kendall
Everyday Acts Against Racism: Raising Children in a Multiracial World – Maureen T. Reddy
Lies My Teacher Told Me – James Loewen
Open Minds to Equality – Nancy Schniedewind and Ellen Davidson – activity book
Prejudice and Your Child – Kenneth B. Clark and Stuart W. Cook
Teaching for Diversity and Social Justice: A Sourcebook for Teachers and Trainers – Maurianne Adams, Lee Ann Bell, and Pat Griffin
Teaching Tolerance: Raising Open-Minded, Empathetic Children – Sam Bullard
Why Are All the Black Kids Sitting Together in the Cafeteria? – Beverly Tatum

Nonfiction

Black Feminist Thought: Knowledge, Consciousness, & the Politics of Empowerment – Patricia Hill Collins
Black Men on Race, Gender, and Sexuality – Devon Carbado
Black Reconstruction in America – W. E. B. DuBois
Black Wealth/White Wealth – Melvin Oliver and Thomas Shapiro
The Damascus Affair – Jonathon Frankel – anti-Semitism
Divided Sisters: Bridging the Gap Between Black Women and White Women – Kathy Wilson and Midge Russell
Fighting Racism in World War II – George Breitmann, C. L. R. James, Fred Stanton, and Ed Keemer
Home Girls: A Black Feminist Anthology – Barbara Smith
Inequality By Design: Cracking the Bell Myth Curve – Claude Fischer et al.
Jews Against Prejudices: American Jews and the Fight for Civil Liberties – Stuart Svonkin
Let's Talk About Racism (The Let's Talk Library) – Diane Shaughnessy
Life, Death, and In-Between on the U.S.-Mexico Border: Asi Es La Vida – Martha Oehmke Loustaunau and Mary-Sanchez Bane
Our Feet Walk the Sky: Women of the South Asian Diaspora – Women of South Asian Descent (Eds.)
Quarantine! – Howard Markel – anti-Semitism

Racial Healing: Confronting the Fear Between Blacks and Whites – Harlon L. Dalton

Racial Politics and the Pedagogy of Whiteness – Henry A. Giroux

Racism Explained to My Daughter – Tahar Ben Jelloun et al.

Sister Outsider – Audre Lorde

Turning Back: The Retreat From Racial Justice in American Thought and Policy – Stephen Steinberg

Women, Race, and Class – Angela Davis

Yo' Mama's Disfunktional: Fighting the Culture Wars in Urban America – Robin D. G. Kelly

Whiteness

A Race is a Nice Thing to Have: A Guide to Being a White Person or Understanding the White Persons in Your Life – Janet Helms

The Universalization of Whiteness: Racism and Enlightenment – Warren Montag

The Wages of Whiteness – David Roediger

White Awareness – Judy Katz

White Women, Race Matters: The Social Construction of Whiteness – Ruth Frankenberg

Spirituality and healing racism

Beyond Fear: Twelve Spiritual Keys to Racial Healing – Aeeshah Ababio Clottey et al.

Enter the River: Healing Steps From White Privilege Toward Racial Reconciliation – Jody Miller Shearer

Pastoral Care: An Antiracist/Multicultural Perspective (Blackwell Studies in Personal and Social Education and Pastoral Care) – Carlton G. Duncan

Anti-racism

Anti-Racism (Key Ideas) – Alastair Bonnett

Dismantling Racism: The Continuing Challenge to White America – Joseph R. Barndt

Fighting Words: Black Women and the Search for Justice – Patricia Hill-Collins

Killing Rage: End Racism – bell hooks
Uprooting Racism: How White People Can Work for Racial Justice – Paul Kivel

Memoirs

The Autobiography of Malcolm X – Malcolm X and Alex Haley
Invisible Privilege: A Memoir About Race, Class, and Gender – Paula S. Rothenberg
Long Time Coming: An Insider's Story of the Birmingham Church Bombing That Rocked the World – Elizabeth H.Cobbs, Petric J. Smith, and Fred L. Shuttlesworth
Narrative of the Life of Frederick Douglass – Frederick Douglass
Night – Elie Weisel – Holocaust
Rising Voices: Writings of Young Native Americans – Arlene B. Hirschfelder and Beverly R. Singer

Fiction

A Lesson Before Dying – Ernest J. Gaines
A Woman of Her Tribe – Margaret Robinson
Beloved – Toni Morrison
Black Boy – Richard Wright
The Bluest Eve – Toni Morrison
The Color Purple – Alice Walker
Dust Tracks on a Road – Zora Neale Hurston
Goodbye Vietnam – Gloria Whelan
Growing Up Chicana/o – Tiffany A. Lopez
I Know Why the Caged Bird Sings – Maya Angelou
Invisible Man – Ralph Ellison
The Joy Luck Club – Amy Tan
The Kitchen God's Wife – Amy Tan
The Latin Deli – Judith Ortiz Cofer
Latina – Lillian Castillo-Speed
Love Medicine – Louise Erdrich
Makes Me Wanna Holler – Nathan McCall
Possessing the Secret of Joy – Alice Walker
Puro Teatro: A Latina Anthology – Alberto Sandoval-Sanchez and Nancy Saporta Sternbach

Their Eyes Were Watching God – Zora Neale Hurston
Things Fall Apart – Chinua Achebe
The Things They Carried – Tim O'Brien
The Wedding – Dorothy West

References

◆ ◆ ◆

Aronson, J. (2002). *Improving academic achievement: Impact of psychological factors on education*. Amsterdam: Academic Press.

Bandura, A. (1965). Influence of models' reinforcement contingencies on the acquisition of imitative responses. *Journal of Personality & Social Psychology, 1*, 589–596.

Bandura, A. (2001). Social cognitive theory: An agentic perspective. *Annual Review of Psychology, 52*, 1–26.

Baumeister, R. F., Campbell, J. D., Krueger, J. I., & Vohs, K. D. (2003). Does high self-esteem cause better performance, interpersonal success, happiness, or healthier lifestyles? *Psychological Science in the Public Interest, 4*(1), 1–44.

Baumrind, D. (1971). Current patterns of parental authority. *Developmental Psychology, 4*(1), 1–103.

Bierman, K. L. (2004). *Peer rejection: Developmental processes and intervention strategies*. New York: Guilford Press.

Billig, S. II. (2000). Research on K-12 school-based service-learning. *Phi Delta Kappan, 81*(9), 658–664.

Bonanno, G. A. (2004). Loss, trauma, and human resilience: Have we underestimated the human capacity to thrive after extremely aversive events? *American Psychologist, 59*(1), 20–28.

Brofenbrenner, U. (1986). Ecology of the family as a context for human development: Resaerch perspectives. *Developmental Psychology, 22*, 723–742.

Brown, J. D. (2002). Mass media influences on sexuality. *Journal of Sex Research, 39*(1), 42.

Buston, K., & Wight, D. (2004). Pupils' participation in sex education lessons: Understanding variation across classes. *Sex Education, 4*(3), 285–301.

Carneiro, P., & Heckman, J. J. (2003). Human capital policy. In J. J. Heckman & A. B. Kruger (Eds.), *Inequality in America: What role for human capital policies?* Cambridge, MA: MIT Press.

Chipuer, H. M. (2001). Dyadic attachments and community connectedness: Links with youths' loneliness experiences. *Journal of Community Psychology, 29*(4), 429–446.

Cochran, M., & Davila, V. (1992). Societal influences on children's peer relationships. In R. D. Parke & G. W. Ladd (Eds.), *Family-peer relationships: Modes of linkage.* (pp. 191–212). Hillsdale, NJ: Lawrence Erlbaum Associates.

Cole, P. M., Martin, S. E., & Dennis, T. A. (2004). Emotion regulation as a scientific construct: Methodological challenges and directions for child development research. *Child Development, 75*(2), 317–333.

Comer, J. P. (2004). *Leave no child behind.* New Haven, CT: Yale University Press.

Csikszentmihalyi, M., & Beattie, O. V. (1979). Life themes: A theoretical and empirical exploration of their origins and effects. *Journal of Humanistic Psychology, 19*(1), 677–693.

Dodge, K. A. (1993). Social cognitive mechanisms in the development of conduct disorder and depression. *Annual Review of Psychology, 44,* 559–584.

Dunn, J. (2004). *Children's friendships: The beginnings of intimacy.* Oxford: Blackwell.

Dynarski, M., Moore, M., Mullens, J., Gleason, P., James-Burdumy, S., Rosenberg, L. et al. (2003). *When schools stay open late: The national evaluation of the 21st-Century Community Learning Centers Program. First year findings.* U.S. Department of Education.

Emde, R. N. (1980). Levels of meaning for infant emotions: A biosocial view. In W. A. Collins (Ed.), *Development of cognition, affect, and social relations.* Hillsdale, NJ: Lawrence Erlbaum Associates.

Endresen, I. M., & Olweus, D. (2005). Participation in power sports and antisocial involvement in preadolescent and adolescent boys. *Journal of Child Psychology and Psychiatry, 46*(5), 468–478.

Englund, M. M., Luckner, A. E., Whaley, G. J. L., & Egeland, B. (2004). Children's achievement in early elementary school: Longitudinal effects of parental involvement, expectations, and quality of assistance. *Journal of Educational Psychology, 96*(4), 723–730.

Flanagan, C. A. (2004). Volunteerism, leadership, political socialization, and civic engagement. In R. M. Lerner & L. Steinberg (Eds.), *Handbook of adolescent psychology* (2nd edn.). Hoboken, NJ: Jonn Wiley & Sons.

Flanagan, C. A., & Tucker, C. J. (1999). Adolescents' explanations for political issues: Concordance with their views of self and society. *Developmental Psychology, 35*(5), 1198–1209.

Fry, W. F. (2002). Humor and the brain: A selective review. *Humor: International Journal of Humor Research, 15*(3), 305–333.

Garmezy, N. (1985). Stress-resistant children: The search for protective factors. In J. E. Stevenson (Ed.), *Recent research in developmental psychopathology* (pp. 213–233). Elsmsford, NY: Pergamon Press.

Gilman, R., Meyers, J., & Perez, L. (2004). Structured extracurricular activities among adolescents: Findings and implications for school psychologists. *Psychology in the Schools, 41*(1), 31–41.

Gniewosz, B., & Noack, P. (2006). Intergenerational transmission and projection processes of intolerant familial attitudes towards foreigners. *Zeitschrift fur Entwicklungspsychologie und Padagogische Psychologie, 38*(1), 33–42.

Grossman, K., & Grossman, K. E. (1985). Maternal sensitivity and newborns' orientation responses as related to quality of attachment in northern Germany. In I. Bretherton & E. Waters (Eds.), *Growing points of attachment: theory and research*. Chicago: University of Chicago Press.

Gruber, H. E., & Voneche, J. J. (Eds.). (1977). *The essential Piaget*. New York: Basic Books.

Grusec, J. E., & Goodnow, J. J. (1994). Impact of parental discipline methods on the child's internalization of values: A reconceptualization of current points of view. *Developmental Psychology, 30*(1), 4–19.

Grusec, J. E., & Kuczynski, L., (Eds.). (1997). *Parenting and children's internalization of values: A handbook of contemporary theory*. New York: John Wiley & Sons, Inc.

Guggenheim, D. (Writer) (2006). An inconvenient truth [video recording]. In L. David, L. Bender, & S. Z. Burns (Producer): Paramount Classics and Participant Productions.

Hall, S. K. (1998). Corporal punishment and the family. *Family Life, 1*, 313–316.

Halpern, D. F. (2005). Psychology at the intersection of work and family: Recommendations for employers, working families, and policymakers. *American Psychologist, 60*(5), 397–409.

Harkness, S., & Super, C. M. (1995). Culture and parenting. In M. H. Bornstein (Ed.), *Handbook of parenting* (Vol. 3). Hillsdale, NJ: Lawrence Erlbaum Associates.

Harrison-Hale, A. O., McLoyd, V. C., & Smedley, B. (2004). Racial and ethnic status: Risk and protective processes among African American families. In K. I. Maton, C. J. Schellenbach, B. J. Leadbeater, & A. L. E. Solarz (Eds.), *Investing in children, youth, families, and communities: Strengths-based research and policy*. Washington, DC: American Psychological Association.

Harter, S. (1989). Self-perception profile for adolescents. Denver: University of Denver, Department of Psychology.

Harter, S. (1999). *The construction of the self*. New York: Guilford Press.

Hearold, S. (1986). A synthesis of 1043 effects of television on social behavior. In G. Comstock (Ed.), *Public communication and behavior* (Vol. 1). New York: Academic Press.

Higher Education Research Institute. (2005). *The American Freshman national norms for Fall 2005*. Los Angeles: Higher Education Research Institute, University of California.

Horng, J.-S., Hong, J.-C., ChanLin, L.-J., Chang, S.-H., & Chu, H.-C. (2005). Creative teachers and creative teaching strategies. *International Journal of Consumer Studies, 29*(4), 352–358.

Kanoy, K., Ulku-Steiner, B., Cox, M., & Burchinal, M. (2003). Marital relationship and individual psychological characteristics that predict physical punishment of children. *Journal of Family Psychology, 17*(1), 20–28.

Kazdin, A. E., & Benjet, C. (2003). Spanking children: Evidence and issues. *Current Directions in Psychological Science, 12*(3), 99–103.

Keltner, D., & Bonanno, G. A. (1997). A study of laughter and dissociation: Distinct correlates of laughter and smiling during bereavement. *Journal of Personality and Social Psychology, 73*(4), 687–702.

Knafo, A. (2003). Contexts, relationship quality, and family value socialization: The case of parent-school ideological fit in Israel. *Personal Relationships, 10*(3), 371–388.

Kochanska, G. (2002). Mutually responsive orientation between mothers and their young children: A context for the early development of conscience. *Current Directions in Psychological Science, 11*(6), 191–195.

Larson, R. W. (2000). Toward a psychology of positive youth development. *American Psychologist, 55*(1), 170–183.

Lefcourt, H. M. (2001). *Humor: The psychology of living buoyantly*. New York: Kluwer Academic.

Lefcourt, H. M., Davidson-Katz, K., & Kueneman, K. (1990). Humor and immune-system functioning. *Humor: International Journal of Humor Research, 3*(3), 305–321.

London, P. (1970). The rescuers: Motivational hypotheses about Christians who saved Jews from the Nazis. In J. Macaulay & L. Berkowitz (Eds.), *Altruism and helping behavior*. New York: Academic Press.

McFarlane, A. C. (1988). Recent life events and psychiatric disorder in children: The interaction with preceding extreme adversity. *Journal of Child Psychology & Psychiatry & Allied Disciplines, 29*(5), 677–690.

McGee, P. E. (1989). *Humor and children's development: A guide to practical applications*. New York: Haworth Press.

Martin, R. A. (1989). Humor and the mastery of living: Using humor to cope with the daily stresses of growing up. In P. E. McGee (Ed.), *Humor and children's development: A guide to practical applications.* New York: Haworth Press.

Martin, R. A. (2001). Humor, laughter, and physical health: Methodological issues and research findings. *Psychological Bulletin, 127*(4), 504–519.

Martin, R. A., & Lefcourt, H. M. (1983). Sense of humor as a moderator of the relation between stressors and moods. *Journal of Personality and Social Psychology, 45*(6), 1313–1324.

Martino, S. C., Collins, R. L., Elliott, M. N., Strachman, A., Kanouse, D. E., & Berry, S. H. (2006). Exposure to degrading versus nondegrading music lyrics and sexual behavior among youth. *Pediatrics, 118*(2), 430–441.

Maruyama, G., Fraser, S. C., & Miller, N. (1982). Personal responsibility and altruism in children. *Journal of Personality and Social Psychology, 42*(4), 658–664.

Masten, A. S. (1986). Humor and competence in school-aged children. *Child Development, 57*(2), 461–473.

Masten, A. S., & Coatsworth, J. D. (1998). The development of competence in favorable and unfavorable environments: Lessons from research on successful children. *American Psychologist, 53*(2), 205–220.

Network, NECCR. (2006). Child-care effect sizes for the NICHD Study of Early Child Care and Youth Development. *American Psychologist, 61*(2), 99–116.

Papousek, H., & Papousek, M. (1992). Beyond emotional bonding: The role of preverbal communication in mental growth and health. *Infant Mental Health Journal, 13*(1), 43–53.

Patrick, H., Turner, J. C., Meyer, D. K., & Midgley, C. (2003). How teachers establish psychological environments during the first days of school: Associations with avoidance in mathematics. *Teachers College Record, 105*(8), 1521–1558.

Puche-Navarro, R. (2004). Graphic jokes and children's mind: An unusual way to approach children's representational activity. *Scandinavian Journal of Psychology, 45*(4), 343–355.

Pyszczynski, T. A., Greenberg, J., Solomon, S., & American Psychological Association. (2003). *In the wake of 9/11: The psychology of terror* (1st edn.). Washington, DC: American Psychological Association.

Regalado, M., Sareen, H., Inkelas, M., Wissow, L. S., & Halfon, N. (2004). Parents' discipline of young children: Results from the national survey of early childhood health. *Pediatrics, 113*, 1952–1958.

Rieger, A., & Ryndak, D. (2004). Explorations of the functions of humor and other types of fun among families of children with disabilities. *Research & Practice for Persons with Severe Disabilities, 29*(3), 194–209.

Rose, S. A. (1994). Relation between physical growth and information processing in infants born in India. *Child Development, 65*(3), 889–902.

Rosenhan, D. (1970). The natural socialization of altruistic autonomy. In J. Macaulay & L. Berkowitz (Eds.), *Altruism and helping behavior*. New York: Academic Press.

Rutter, M. (1979). Protective factors in children's response to stress and disadvantage. In M. W. K. J. E. Rolf (Ed.), *Primary prevention in psychopathology* (Vol. 3). Hanover: University of New Hampshire Press.

Rutter, M., & O'Connor, T. G. (2004). Are there biological programming effects for psychological development? Findings from a study of Romanian adoptees. *Developmental Psychology, 40*(1), 81–94.

Saarni, C. (1999). *The development of emotional competence*. New York: Guilford Press.

Santrock, J. W. (2007). *Adolescence* (11th edn.). Boston: McGraw Hill.

Seligman, M. E. P. (1991). *Learned optimism*. New York: Knopf.

Shatz, M., & Gelman, R. (1973). The development of communication skills: Modifications in the speech of young children as a function of listener. *Monographs of the Society for Research in Child Development, 38*(5), 1–37.

Smetana, J. G., & Metzger, A. (2005). Family and religious antecedents of civic involvement in middle class African American late adolescents. *Journal of Research on Adolescence, 15*(3), 325–352.

Smith, A., Schneider, B., & Ruck, M. (2005). "Thinking About Makin' It": Black Canadian students' beliefs regarding education and academic achievement. *Journal of Youth & Adolescence, 34*(4), 347–359.

Smith, S. L., & Donnerstein, E. (1998). Harmful effects of exposure to media violence: Learning of aggression, emotional desensitization, and fear. In R. Green & E. Donnerstein (Eds.), *Human aggression: Theories, research and implications for social policy*. New York: Academic Press.

Spelke, E. S. (2002). Developmental neuroimaging: A developmental psychologist looks ahead. *Developmental Science, 5*(3), 392–396.

Steele, C. M., & Aronson, J. (1995). Stereotype threat and the intellectual test performance of African Americans. *Journal of Personality and Social Psychology, 69*(5), 797–811.

Steinberg, L. (2004). *The ten basic principles of good parenting*. New York: Simon & Schuster.

Stevenson, H. W., & Lee, S.-Y. (1990). Contexts of achievement: A study of American, Chinese, and Japanese children. *Monographs of the Society for Research in Child Development, 55*.

Strage, A. (2004). Long-term academic benefits of service-learning: When and where do they manifest themselves? *College Student Journal, 38*(2), 257–261.

Straus, M., Gelles, R., & Steinmetz, S. (1980). *Behind closed doors: Violence in the American family.* New York: Doubleday.

Strayer, J., & Roberts, W. (2004). Children's anger, emotional expressiveness, and empathy: Relations with parents' empathy, emotional expressiveness, and parenting practices. *Social Development, 13*(2), 229–254.

Trevlas, E., Matsouka, O., & Zachopoulou, E. (2003). Relationship between playfulness and motor creativity in preschool children. *Early Child Development & Care, 173*(5), 535–543.

Triandis, H. C. (1994). *Culture and social behavior.* New York: McGraw-Hill.

Van Ijzendoorn, M. H., & Kroonenberg, P. M. (1988). Cross-cultural patterns of attachment: A meta-analysis of Strange Situation. *Child Development, 59*(1), 147–156.

Vygotsky, L. S. (1962). *Thought and language.* Cambridge, MA: MIT Press.

Weinstein, G., & Obear, K. (1992). Bias issues in the classroom: Encounters with the teaching self. In M. E. Adams (Ed.), *Promoting diversity in college classrooms: Innovative responses for the curriculum, faculty, and institutions,* New Directions for Teaching and Learning, no. 52. (pp. 39–50). San Francisco: Jossey-Bass.

Werner, E. E., & Smith, R. S. (1982). *Vulnerable but invincible longitudinal study of resilient children and youth.* New York: McGraw-Hill.

Wesley, J. (1915). *Letters of John Wesley.* London: Hodder and Stoughton.

Winstead, B. A. (2004). Social networks and social support in childhood and adolescence. *PsycCritiques.*

Xiao, H. (2000). Class, gender, and parental values in the 1990s. *Gender and Society, 14*(6), 785–803.

Index

LaVergne, TN USA
17 December 2009
167382LV00003B/5/P